Dear Kathleen,

You are the best. That's all.

Love,

Daryl

THE PARENTS' GUIDE TO
CAREER PLANNING
FOR YOUR TWENTYSOMETHING

THE PARENTS' GUIDE TO

CAREER PLANNING

FOR YOUR TWENTYSOMETHING

How Parents Can Help Their College and
Post-College Age Children Find Careers That Lead
to HAPPINESS and SUCCESS

DARYL CAPUANO

Daryl Capuano

Student Mastery Publishing

Copyright 2019

Student Mastery Publishing

Old Saybrook, CT

ISBN: 978-0-98494-512-2 (print)

ISBN: 978-0-98494-513-9 (ebook)

To my father, without whom, my happy career would not be possible. To Francie, Danny, Kearney, and Katie, without whom, my happy life would not be possible.

TABLE OF CONTENTS

PREFACE:

WHO IS THIS BOOK FOR?

The main 21st century shift for parents:

You are still needed beyond college acceptance

AFTER SUFFERING THROUGH THE TEEN YEARS, YOUR CHILD WAS finally accepted to college. In addition to the joy you felt about the accomplishment of college admission and the hope that they would have a wonderful life experience, you also likely felt the relief of a burden being lifted.

Sure, you would still worry about all the things that parents worry about forever—are my children happy, healthy, and in good relationships? But the big practical burden—"What will they do when they grow up?" was relieved. Your boy or girl went off to college. They would figure out their work lives from there.

No? That didn't happen? You are not alone.

"College" Does Not Provide Career Guidance

Despite the radical change in college to career transitions that have occurred in the last few decades, parents still tend to conflate the college decision with the career decision: "Once we get Johnny off to *college*, he'll figure out his *career*." This misguided thinking was never quite right. Even in the go-go 80s and 90s, colleges did a lousy job of career preparation. But the work world revolution of the last few decades has exacerbated the problem. Economic realities—not an extension of helicoptering parents—have created the need for greater parental involvement with career issues.

I run The Learning Consultants, the largest private educational consultancy in Connecticut. The number of parents who have called seeking advice for their college-age children has multiplied exponentially in the last ten years, so much so that I created 'Career Counseling Connecticut' to focus exclusively on career advisory services. My last book *Career Path of Abundance* connected me with readers who lived across the US and, surprisingly, with many English-speaking readers across the world. Those that live far away and would prefer not to meet virtually would ask, "What can I do for my children?" That's what this book addresses. What can parents do to help their children find happy and successful careers?

Almost every career book is for the career seeker, often of varied ages. But this book is for parents trying to help their college or post-college age child transition effectively into a happy and successful career. The genesis of the book sprung from career counseling work with parents who felt helpless as they watched their twentysomething children struggle with career issues. This guide will help parents help their children navigate the increasingly complex world of career choices. If the readers of this book are typical of our company's clients, they are the parents of:

(1) young adults who graduated from college but have not found work that has placed them on a career path of their choice

(2) college students or those who have had an interrupted college experience who are facing the college-to-career transition

(3) high school students, who, prior to investing in college, want to have a conversation about choosing their career

Certainly, some parts of the book—particularly, areas related to what I call 'The New World of Work'—can and should be read by young adult career seekers and Part II: The College to Career Program is designed specifically to help jump-start the how-to find a career process. But I am writing the majority of this book as if I was meeting with our parent-clients, as opposed to our student-clients.

I should also be clear about what "guidance" will be provided. This is not a book about resumes, cover letters, networking, interviewing and other tactics related to career issues. There is a plethora of resources that cover such subjects. Instead, this is a big picture book of lessons that will help parents help their children with the question that often is still not answered upon growing up: ***"What do you want to do when you grow up?"***

INTRODUCTION:

THERE IS ALWAYS HOPE

"I want to help but I just don't know how."

SO, BEGAN A TYPICAL DAY.

I listened as Barbara described her 24-year-old son. Kyle had graduated with a degree in film studies from a good private college. He had done well in high school. His grades in college were solid. He was likable and creative. He had fun in college but was not a big partier.

Barbara was bewildered by Kyle's current situation. Two years after college, Kyle's career was still adrift. Other than a few part-time jobs, one in retail and the other at a proverbial coffee shop, he had developed no career building experience. He did not have a history of depression. But over the last year, he was growing increasingly anxious and depressed. She was terrified of a potential downward spiral.

I met Kyle shortly thereafter for our first career counseling session. Introverted, but not overly so, a bit wary initially but forthcoming soon enough, he relayed his story. He was a good student in high school and was happy to gain admission to a reasonably high ranked college. He had not thought too much about what he wanted to do for his career. That seemed far away. When pressed, he would say, "It would be great to go to Hollywood and make movies," and then knowingly laugh as he knew that sounded naïve.

During his first year of college, Kyle grappled with adjusting to the freshman year. Some ups and downs but nothing out of the ordinary. He still didn't really know what he wanted to do post-college and, while he tried to not think about the issue, he was growing a bit anxious.

In the middle of sophomore year, Kyle had to declare a major. He ruled out majoring in one of the typical liberal arts fields. "I knew I didn't want to be an English or history major." Kyle recalled his college advisor asking him. "What are you passionate about?" Kyle wasn't really sure but he liked his freshman year 'Introduction to Film Studies' and he liked the titles of other courses in the film department. He noted, "'Classic Films Depicting the 1960s' sounded more interesting than 'Shakespeare's Sonnets' so I decided to major in film."

I asked Kyle what his parents thought about his film major. "They always told me that I should find what I want to do." So, Kyle didn't think that his decision would cause a problem at home until he told his father. "He kind of flipped out, which surprised me. He asked what I was going to do with a film degree but he didn't have an answer when I said, 'What am I going to do with an English degree?' My mom got on the phone, calmed us both down, and then we just didn't talk about it again."

During his freshman and sophomore summers, Kyle worked in a clothing store at a nearby mall. There did not seem to be any need to build his career. Other than some of his business-focused acquaintances, most of his buddies did something similar.

As a junior, Kyle heard it was important to get an internship for the summer. He felt fortunate to get a six-week unpaid gig, working on an independent film as a production assistant. He realized a few things during the internship. First, his academic training in film studies was not really helpful at all in film production. He did not have the skills required to be much more than a gopher on set. Second, the artsy independent film making crew was not really his people. Kyle was suburban cultured, not 'filled with tattoos and earrings' as he described. Third, Kyle had a better sense of the economic challenges faced by those who take this path. In his words, "There was a mix of rich kids whose parents funded them and real artists who didn't mind sleeping in their cars. I knew I wasn't either and I realized that I wouldn't be going to Hollywood to make movies."

During senior year, Kyle buried his head in the sand in relation to pending thoughts of graduation and the real world. "I was just trying to get through it." Since many of his film studies classmates—indeed, many of his classmates—were similarly undirected, Kyle did not feel pressured.

I asked Kyle about his discussions with his parents during this time. "They didn't want to put pressure on me, although I had the sense that my Dad was getting edgy about the subject. Kyle did not apply for jobs during his senior year. "I thought I would figure it out when I graduated." A decade ago, I would have been surprised by that comment. But I have heard this story so often that I no longer am. Many college seniors are not engaged in intense job searches. Similarly, I am no longer surprised that many parents do not engage in conversations with the college-age students about the work world. I will address the reasons soon enough.

When Kyle graduated in May of his senior year, he "decompressed" until after July 4th weekend. Then, with the thought of just making some money for a couple months went back to his old summer job at the mall. While he always intellectually understood that he didn't have a post-graduation plan, he now emotionally understood as well. He started sending out resumes in early August to jobs posted on job search engines such as Indeed and Monster. He discovered, as do many, that these search engines are often black holes where resumes and applications disappear to never be heard from again.

Kyle applied for a variety of entry-level jobs that either sparked his interest, even if he did not have a relevant background, or were loosely related to film or video. As the Fall arrived, he became anxious. His parents did as well and started peppering him with suggestions, often at times when he was trying to relax. This led to some heated exchanges and then periods of time not talking about his plans.

Working at the mall during the summer felt temporary and not part of his identity when Kyle was a student. But now that he was no longer a student, he felt beaten down when he went to his mall job. After the Christmas holidays, the store did not need him other than to substitute for its regular full-year staff. He was completely out of work for a month and felt lucky to get a job through his mom's friend at a local coffee shop where he had worked 20-30 hours per week for a year and a half before our meeting.

During this time, Kyle would have spurts of applying for jobs in a similar fashion as before, get frustrated, and then stop. His relationship with his father had deteriorated. "I come home after a day of working at the coffee shop, which doesn't sound hard to him but it is real work and tiring. If I'm playing video games or watching NetFlix, he makes some crack about my tough life. It got to the point that I just don't want to be around him."

Kyle concluded his story with a common refrain: "I feel hopeless."

The contours of Kyle's situation are not that different than many twentysomethings, who, despite having graduated college - once a near guarantee for gainful employment -, are unemployed or underemployed.

Yet, we are also in a New World of Work. As will be described throughout the book, we are in a work revolution that is as large in scope as the Industrial Revolution. While there are distinct challenges within this new world, there is also dramatically more potential to create far more work happiness than ever before. Through a process of creating a general, even if loose, vision of a realistic career path that will lead to both happiness and success, creating a plan to build skills, credentials, and experience that connect to the path, and then executing an effective job search-career building plan in twenty-first century fashion, Kyle and others have the capacity to not only get a job and get on a career path but to have far more vibrant work lives than those in previous generations.

Kyle and his parents asked if there was any hope.

There is always hope.

Why the enhanced need for career advice from parents?

I started providing career counseling services before The Great Recession of 2007-09. Even then, most of our recent college graduate clients had experienced some form of post-collegiate misery. Many had entry-level jobs where the biggest lesson was discovering what they hated. Others were floating in transitional stages. I felt particularly bad for those students who had done "the right things". They worked hard in school. They suffered for their good grades. The payoff was supposed to happen when they got into the work world. Back then, when there were plenty of career building jobs for recent college grads, many had landed prestigious and high paying entry-level positions. But a fair amount had sought out what they perceived as a top job without giving much thought—and through getting poor advice—about what jobs would suit them.

Consequently, I would meet unhappy financial analysts who had been told Wall St. was the answer or disillusioned law school students or management consultants who did not realize that their life would be consumed by air travel. Likewise, other prestigious post-collegiate steps were not working out for many of my clients. Each of those options was and is wonderful for some. The problem for my clients was the mismatch between the so-called plum job and their particular interests, values, and preferences.

But the career crisis for young adults has been magnified exponentially due to the restructured post-Great Recession economy. There is a far greater need to not only find a career match among many options but to simply find a career building job.

Moreover, the resources for parents and children alike on the subject have been scarce or ineffective.

Adult Advisors

Adult advisors who are put on the spot to provide informal career counseling are usually not effective. The main reason: they are compelled to be glib, quickly giving advice based on their limited knowledge of the broad marketplace, personal biases, and often superficial understanding of the young career seeker. In most scenarios, the well-meaning adult provides thoughts while in an informal setting and does not have the time to thoughtfully account for all the unique factors of the career seeker. I made this mistake years ago. I was at a party when a friend approached me for career advice for her twentysomething daughter. "What do you think of X career?" she asked. I found myself doing what most do; I immediately answered the question in an effort to be helpful. About twenty minutes later, I heard my friend tell her daughter, "Daryl said…." I suddenly realized that I made a terrible mistake. I didn't ask questions about her daughter. I knew nothing about her values, interests, core motivations and personality preferences. Yet, I was being quoted as an authoritative voice that could affect her decision-making process. I resolved then to answer such questions thoughtfully or not answer unless I was engaged in a meaningful interaction.

Yet, many of my young adult clients tell me that their uncle or mom's friend or professor gave some generic advice that they thought was worth following. The most common advice stems from the successful adult sharing a success story and suggesting that the young adult might want to follow a similar path. This "advice" might be helpful if, coincidentally, the young adult has a similar personality/psychology and, in the unlikely event, that the industry has not shifted much since the older success entered the field a couple decades ago. The advice might be decidedly unhelpful and potentially disastrous if those factors are not in place.

While at college, the most common adult advisor is a helpful professor. Professors are experts in history or psychology or marketing. They are usually very smart. But they are not, and, rarely pretend to be, career advisors. Unfortunately, students have so few resources to turn to for career advice that their professors are often the only adult resources they have on campus. When I hear one of our career counseling clients say "my professor suggested that I look into...", I usually cringe. The professor was most-likely a well-meaning educator trying to help the student but might not have realized that the suggestion of a trusted professor would translate into "the authority told me I should...". Most academics have only been in the education world. For the most part, they went to graduate school after college and then began their professorial careers. Much like anyone who is a specialist, they know little about other areas of work life and lack a broad-based knowledge regarding the variety of careers, particularly those most relevant today not twenty years ago.

Career Services

College career services provide a false sense of security for parents. Most are designed as career placement services. There is a huge difference between placement and advisory services. The mandate for career placement is to get employers to interview students on campus and to help get their students employed. This is an incredibly valuable service. But typically, most do not focus on helping individual students figure out their career paths. They simply do not have the time for such customized work.

Unhelpful Career Books

Over the years, I have read dozens of career advisory books. This study related not only to my work providing career advisory services but also in relation to my own career transition. Much of the literature requires a tangible understanding of the work world in order to be engaged in the material. This is not helpful for many young adults.

Most other books geared for young adults are broad overviews of hundreds of careers. These books provided a starting point for career discussions. But the books are not designed, or perhaps are designed poorly, to help readers sort out what career is uniquely suited for the student. The overview books typically provide a couple paragraph generalization about a career. Most, however, lack the sophistication to help young adults make career decisions. In addition, the rapidly changing world of work has made most such books outdated.

Of recent vintage, the most common theme for career books emanates from the follow your passion movement. Unfortunately, too many of these books disproportionately focus on passion over economic practicality. Indeed, the barrage of follow your passion treatises has created unintended pressure on young adults to find their work passion—which is more rare than common—or to have such an unrealistic understanding of the work world that disillusionment sets in quite hard.

. . . .

MAIN TAKEAWAY:
There are few resources that help young adults figure out career choice.

PART I:

LESSONS FOR PARENTS

LESSON 1:

OVERCOMING DEAD POET'S SOCIETY SYNDROME

"I DON'T THINK WE SHOULD GET INVOLVED. IT'S HIS LIFE AND his career."

Kyle's mom said when I asked her about her discussions with Kyle about his career.

I have heard variations of this phrase hundreds of times now and realize that it is part of the good parent playbook of our generation.

Popular culture has demonized overbearing parents and probably rightly so based upon the caricatures of the stifling culture of prior generations. The boss-parent model was savaged in TV shows, after-school specials, as well as movies in the 80s and 90s. Storylines of demanding parents lording over their children to follow their expectations, including career aspirations, became cliché.

Parents of millennials developed what I call *Dead Poet's Society Syndrome*. With hope, the movie has been around long enough that I don't need to provide a spoiler alert... In a prep school setting in the late 1950s, a heroic teacher inspires students to live passionately. In response, the main teen character embraces acting as his intended profession instead of medicine, as his parents expected. His demanding father pressures his son to give up theatre. Disastrous consequences follow. That parent type still exists but has—fortunately—become a distinct minority.

Prior parental generations were overbearing by our standards. Many children ignored their authentic career aspirations to fit family expectations. But, as tends to happen with most philosophical swings, the pendulum swung too far. In a well-meaning effort to let our children follow their dreams, the current generation of parents has largely abdicated their role as sensible advice givers. Current conventional parental philosophy has shifted to "let your children do what they want." Parents will often reflexively say they do not want to interfere with their children's career goals. This removes the gift that comes from having wise parents. Effectively guiding is different than interfering.

I am well aware of the immediate rebuttal: "What about all that I've read about helicopter parents?" In my observation of thousands of parents through the years, I concur that parents step in to solve day to day problems on a scale that is significantly higher than years past and often in an unhealthy way. Parent involvement with challenges related to their children's relationships, academics, and activities has become out of control. New terms for this phenomenon—bull-dozer or snow plow parents—capture the way that hovering parents of young children, the helicopering type, grow into removing the obstacles in their older children's lives. This includes doing things that I would never recommend in a career context such as contacting employers or filling in job applications.

Nonetheless, in my experience, most parents do not make decisions about what their children should do for their careers. That is a very good development. But most parents also do not provide much guidance on the subject either. This has contributed to career challenges faced by twentysomethings.

Well-meaning parents worry that giving advice might create a challenge for their parent-child relationship. In relation to major life issues, it is the "how" parents get involved not the "should" that creates problems. If it was clear that your son's serious girlfriend had a drinking problem, you could bark at the wrong moment, "Break up with that drunk." Or you could figure out the tactful way to approach the subject and then discuss the matter empathetically. It would be irresponsible to let him drift into marriage without addressing the issue.

This trend does not stem solely from the shifting of parental philosophies. In the last of couple decades, there has also been an enormous increase in the energetic investment that parents put into helping their children gain admission to college. That investment makes sense, given both the massive life shift that college presents and the amount of money college costs. But part of that energetic investment stems from the pervasive but flawed view that the student-child will figure out what to do for work in college and, the even more inaccurate expectation, that college will guide the student to an optimal career choice.

We told our children they can do whatever they want.

"That's up to him."

So said a very well-meaning set of baby-boomer parents simultaneously. We were discussing their seventeen-year-old son Kevin and what he might want to study in college.

Kevin looked and sounded completely bewildered. While he was encouraged to do whatever he wanted, Kevin had no context to understand the work world. High school curriculums provide the bare minimum exposure to potential career options. Kevin's life experience was that of a typical sheltered suburbanite. Like many teens, he didn't really understand what his parents did for work. When asked, he responded, "My Dad travels a lot for business but I'm not sure what he does and my mom works in an office." His response was fairly typical. Outside of the professions that they see in person—doctor, nurse, teacher, policeman, fireman and so forth—young adults have a limited understanding of careers unless they are educated by their parents.

Kevin's parents were extremely nice. Their decision to let their son gravitate towards what he wanted to do did not stem from neglect but rather from a desire to avoid pressuring him. But in doing so, like many parents, they had done nothing to guide or otherwise educate their son about the world of work. At least, Kevin had time on his side.

The tougher calls are from parents with post-college children.

"We told Andrea to follow her passion but she's finding out there are not many jobs for dance majors."

I am all for those that follow non-traditional paths. But those that do have to be highly educated on the battle they will face to find sustainable work. Dance majors shouldn't be surprised at age 22 that finding full-time employment in an area unrelated to dance will be difficult.

"David studied finance but really hates it."

In David's case, he was following a traditional route but when I asked him why he chose finance, he noted—as do a surprisingly high number of my young clients—that his buddies suggested doing so. Look at your children's friends. They will be the prime influencers of their lives if you are not. Moreover, high school guidance counselors, college professors, and other adults are rarely influential in our increasingly bubbled world. Few live in a "village" environment where town elders will provide guidance. If you do not provide guidance, then perhaps no one—or perhaps no one you want—will.

Like it or not, you are your children's main advisor.

Most Colleges Do Not Provide Career *Exploration*

The illusion that colleges helped students figure out what they wanted to do for their careers was created during strong economic times. Colleges provide training grounds in certain career disciplines for those who already know what they want to do and the more elite colleges attract employers to come to campus and hire their students. But colleges have never spent considerable energy helping students figure out what they wanted to do post-college.

For many, it simply appeared that college students figured out what to do in college because from the 1960s through the early 2000s there was an abundance of career building jobs for most all recent college graduates. This is no longer the case.

That is the build-up for "why you should get involved." Those who already are convinced can move on to the next lesson. In my experience, however, many parents need additional convincing if only to battle through their internal resistance. The next few pages lay out an extended case for why you should get involved with your child's career because you will need to convince yourself to muster the energy to do so. Energy generation should not be underestimated. Many parents give up trying to help because the stress of getting involved is draining. Quitting is not the answer, particularly when it comes to parenting.

Parents Should Help Their Children... Always

Let's start off with some counterintuitive wisdom. Your child is not too old to get practical guidance from you. You are not interfering. You are not being a helicopter parent. You are doing what parents do throughout their entire lives. You are guiding them. This is not unusual. By historical standards, we are the strange ones.

Throughout history, parents guided children about work and life well into adulthood. Farmer is the most common occupation in human history. If we generalize about gender roles back then, young male farmers worked next to their fathers until they took over the family farm. And, even if that was in young adulthood, which was not likely, fathers would continually provide practical guidance on how best to plant, plow, and harvest crops. Similarly, mothers would continue to give their adult daughters or wives of their sons, guidance on running the other areas of the farmer's house.

The same process occurred for merchants, craftsmen, and others in family-owned businesses. Only since the Industrial Revolution and, even then, only so in the corporatization of the work world, has it become common for adults to work in entirely different fields than their parents. So *no*, you are not being an overbearing parent by giving advice. That's the parent's role and that role should continue as long as the parent can be helpful.

Failure to launch has become a commonality not a rarity

There is an even simpler answer: necessity. The inability of young adults to gain career traction is unprecedented in the modern Western world creating a brutally tough emotional and practical challenge for parents. Their college graduate or soon to be college graduate or interrupted college-age child is not financially independent. The old school way of thinking—not your problem, let your child deal with the real world—is not the optimal answer. Many of these twentysomethings generally acted responsibly through college—or at least not much different than their parents - and equally want to gain financial independence. Few are happy about having to live back at home and/or take supplemental money from their parents.

If you need additional ammunition to get you started, here are the reasons to get involved:

(1) Importance

Some areas of life are so vital that parents should advise their children even as adults. Marriage, parenthood, health, and career are profoundly connected to overall life happiness. Unless you think your parental duties end when your children leave the house, you should provide guidance in each of these areas if possible. It is worth reiterating that problems occur because of "how" the advice is given. If you learn to effectively guide, your children will want to come to you for advice.

(2) Rational time, energy, and financial investment analysis

The investment that parents make to ensure the high school to college transition makes sense. Parents spend an enormous amount of time, money, and energy ensuring that their children get into the right college. College is a major turning point in life and, in the developed world, college is the transition to adulthood.

Yet, most parents spend a minimal amount of time, money, and energy ensuring that their children get into the right career. This makes no sense. Careers are forty to fifty (maybe even sixty for this generation) years. And, careers aren't just turning points in life but life itself.

That, alone, is sufficient justification for all parents to help guide their children. But as the remainder of the book will elaborate upon, we are in extraordinary economic times. The world of work is quite possibly more unpredictable than at any time in human history. We are in a work revolution. Consider that until the Industrial Revolution most everyone was a farmer, a tradesman, a soldier, a seaman, a merchant or a manual laborer (including slaves). Today, many young people and their parents do not even know how to describe many jobs in the ever evolving technology oriented workplace.

(3) Psychological well-being

Self-esteem is highly connected to career. Twentysomethings who have floundering careers are more likely to drift or plummet down the psychological wormhole. Given the epidemic of depression and anxiety in our society, ensuring that your children have happy and successful careers is an important way to protect against mental health issues.

This issue cannot be underestimated. Social media has had many unintended consequences. While there has been extensive societal discussion about the distraction created by social media, there has not been sufficient discussion about detrimental social comparisons. When I work with college students who want to transfer, many say that "everyone is having fun at their colleges but me." I point out that their friends at other colleges are not posting the hours they are alone in their room but snippets from the thirty minutes of the wildest time they had during the week. The same is true for those who post about their careers. My young adult clients will lament that "everyone knows what they want to do." I will note that the thousands without good jobs are not posting about their work but that only a few with great jobs are. Still, a picture is worth a thousand words. It is hard to battle with an onslaught of imagery that makes one feel badly in comparison.

(4) Financial Independence for your child

Financial necessity is the most tangible reason for getting involved with your child's career path. While our first world focus on psychological well-being and other ethereal factors related to career are important, the primary reason for work for most people in the world is financial independence.

Contrary to any thought that young adults are happy to take money from their parents, most of my young clients suffer over doing so and desperately want to cut the financial strings from their parents.

(5) Guidance is needed

Your advice is not superfluous. You will not be giving counsel related to something your children understand or can figure out on their own. The work world is dramatically different than back in our day. "He'll figure it out" used to be translated into "someone will hire him" and then he will be on his way. That's not the case anymore. One of the reasons why parents do not guide their children in the college-career transition is lack of knowledge on how to do so. Many parents have also been negatively affected by what I label as "the New World of Work." They are grappling with what is happening to their own careers. We are living in enormously confusing times. With hope, this book will not only help you guide your children but also help you guide yourself.

(6) Career development only gets harder with the passage of time

Developing a viable career path gets harder as time passes. Too many twentysomethings started post-college unemployment with the thought that they'll get on a career track after the summer of graduation. The summer often becomes a year. After a year or two, a whole host of factors make it more difficult to gain career traction. The most significant is that the headline on their resume no longer starts with their educational history but with their restaurant or retail store jobs.

There is also the danger of a mismatched job. If your child has a job that is not a long term fit, then she will need to move on sooner than later. Otherwise, she will be branding herself in a career that doesn't suit her. Years ago, during the heyday of Wall Street, one of my clients—an English major from an Ivy League school who had no background in finance—interviewed, on a whim, for a finance job. Since she was extremely bright and personable, she was hired for an entry-level investment banking job. She took the job because of the high salary. She hated it from the start, but stuck out two years in order to build her resume with work experience. When she applied for jobs in publishing, this life-long reader-writer-English major was told by numerous employers that her financial background indicated she was a bad fit for the publishing industry.

(7) Marriage and grandchildren

Lack of career stability has become the dominant reason why young adults do not start families. This is still a gender tilted issue. Suffice to say, men generally push off marriage—and fatherhood—until they feel settled into a career. This is a trend that will have serious effects on society.

I worked with Jack, a twenty-eight year-old, who had drifted through his early twenties post-college with a series of non-career building jobs and bouts of unemployment. He wanted to start a family and had a serious girlfriend that he wanted to marry. But he thought—and many would agree—that it made sense to figure out the career issue before doing so.

(8) Better relationship with your adult child

Assuming you can figure out the *how*—the default being sending them for professional advisory services—you will build your relationship in a healthy way: You will be the wise mentor. The bittersweet sting of having children leave home and move on creates deep melancholy. If you can be a guide in your adult child's life, you will develop another facet for your relationship to continue in a healthy way.

(9) Ensuring your financial resources are protected

Your resources will be drained if your children are not financially independent. Parents will often spend their last dollars on their children and some of my clients are doing so. That will not serve anyone. Parents often are selfless when helping their children. But there are several factors that should push against this urge. While it is a whole other subject, we are facing an inevitable macro crisis as the median retirement savings of those nearing retirement age is woefully inadequate, years in retirement are increasing, and standard retirement vehicles, such as pensions, are disappearing.

Ensuring your children are on a proper career path will be a better investment strategy than properly allocating your 401k investments.

(10) Purposefulness for you

Elders in other societies and in other time periods were venerated. Their wisdom and experience were valued. They had a purpose for the tribe, clan, and village, in part because they could give helpful advice to guide others. In modern Western societies, this is not the case. While I am not suggesting that you manage your adult child's career, I am suggesting that you continue to help your child as long as you are able. And this will also help provide meaning in your life if you can become an effective advisor.

My main company, The Learning Consultants, focuses upon helping high school students gain admission to college. For that reason, I know a large number of parents, particularly moms, who would curse the amount of stress related to the college process. When I bump into some of them a few years later, many seemed profoundly sad and would tell me that they preferred the purposefulness of guiding, even when stressful, to feeling less than useful.

. . . .

MAIN POINT:

Our current cultural programming may be limiting
you from helping your child.

LESSON 2:

DON'T BE A FARMER IN THE INDUSTRIAL REVOLUTION

"WE WANT CAITLYN TO GET A FULL-TIME JOB WITH BENEFITS IN some place where she can work her way up the ladder."

Caitlyn had a degree in environmental studies. Heading into the "Green Industry" is a perfectly viable plan. But Caitlyn had zero interest in the science related to environmentalism. She also had no real knowledge about sustainability or any other semi-technical area where there are jobs for environmental studies majors. She also had no knowledge and seemingly no interest in businesses within the environmental sector.

When I asked her about skills that she had or wanted to develop, she looked at me blankly and replied, "I have a degree." I responded, "I understand but how will you contribute or how do you want to contribute to an organization?" "I just want to get hired and then do whatever work they give me." Caitlyn continued. I then walked her through the normal operations of an organization from finance-accounting through sales-marketing and everything in-between. She looked at me perplexed and noted that she never thought about any of these areas.

I explained that not having any skills was a problem but not an insurmountable one. We simply had to figure out what she wanted to develop so that she could contribute to an organization. Then we had to craft a plan to develop those skills through either self-education, formal training, or internships. More importantly, we had to convey to potential employers what she wanted to do. Caitlyn's mom interjected, "I told her that most companies will hire her, find out what she likes to do and then train her." I wanted to say "1990s are calling..."

I have sympathy for Caitlyn's mom. She had not been in the workforce since Caitlyn's older brother was born twenty-five years ago. In that time, the work world radically changed. Today, her words sound extraordinarily naïve—at least to those who are in the New World of Work— but from her 1980s-1990s perspective it was entirely possible to get hired by large organizations, rotate through departments, find a fit, get trained, and then work one's way upward. Such opportunities still exist, particularly for those graduating from elite colleges, but are now few and far between.

The New World of Work

Revolution may seem to be a dramatic word for a couple decade plus gradual process. But in historical terms, The Information Age Revolution represents a far more tumultuous upheaval of the old order than the seventy-five year plus Industrial Revolution. Why does this matter? Because much of what you thought you knew about the work world is no longer correct and, as is the thesis of this book, since you are your children's main source of guidance, your children might get lost in the tumult unless you help.

If you are a parent in the early 21st century, you are in the sandwich generation of the revolution. Your parents—and your original cultural understanding about careers—were part of the Old World of Work. That world was relatively predictable, at least by our standards. Your children will be part of the New World of Work. You are living through the transition and much like all areas of growth need to move through the uncomfortableness of foregoing outdated beliefs.

The sandwich generation was conditioned that they and their children would have:

(1)   full-time jobs

(2)   with benefits

(3)   into the indefinite future

(4)   on a distinct and life-long career path

(5)   most likely with large organizations and usually with one organization for a lengthy time

My original programming was exactly the same. My father put himself through college and graduate school and worked for a large multi-national company for over thirty years. He rose through the ranks to an executive position, developed life-long friends and a vibrant community of colleagues, and retired with an extraordinary pension. There was a linear template to follow: gain admission to institutions of higher learning, get hired by big business and climb the corporate ladder. His American Dream story—much like many of those who were fortunate to enter the workforce during the greatest economic boom in modern history—will be increasingly rare.

In no way does the economic good fortune of my father's generation diminish the hard work and talent of those that followed this path successfully. There were plenty in his day who were derailed. But, for most, the reasons for their challenging circumstances were more understandable within the context of a meritocracy. They did not pursue higher education or they did not work hard in school or did not work hard in their career. And, of course, many were just not that talented in ways that led to successful careers. Today, the career road is far more mercurial. Most anyone—even those who "do the right things" and have talent—can suffer, often mightily, at the hands of macroeconomic fate.

The New World of Work Revolution

In the Old World of Work, the path was predictable: Graduate from college, find the first job in a chosen career field with perhaps a move or two to find the right organization and then embark on a long-time stay at that organization. Even the somewhat aimless or initially misdirected would usually find their career traction sometime in their mid to late twenties.

When I give talks on this subject, I often mention that when I graduated college in 1989, most anyone with decent grades from a decent college would find a decent job. I see heads nodding for anyone who graduated college before the mid-2000s.

Furthermore, career paths for most were also predictable, particularly for those in the world of organizations. Upon joining a company in an entry-level position, one would strive for upward mobility. Career paths could easily be viewed on an organizational chart: Assistant manager to associate manager to senior manager to assistant director to associate director and so on. There was a reasonable amount of predictability about moving through each of these points within three to seven years. Upward mobility would continue for some and stop for others.

Moving to a different department within the same company was considered a big career move. Taking a similar job in a different company was a huge—and somewhat risky—career move. Those who switched careers were considered highly unusual, often not in a good way. Those in professions or other specialized fields had their own paths, but, for the most part, those paths were similarly predictable.

For those in large, reasonably stable organizations who have not yet felt the sting of job disruption, the illusion of the Old World of Work remains. The misconception stems from not realizing that the pact of committing oneself to a corporation in exchange for secure employment into the indefinite future no longer exists. For workers who have experienced the effects of the New World of Work, thoughts of lifetime employment have already faded away.

This Is Not About Recent Economic Challenges but Dramatic Economic Change

The financial tailspin of the first decade of the twenty-first century accelerated—but did not cause—the dramatic structural shifts that were already happening in the economy. Changes were afoot well before 2008's meltdown. I note this point because some in our generation have a lingering hope that the work world will snap back into predictable order even though The Great Recession is a decade in the past. The Internet revolution of the 1990s both decimated and created entire industries. In 1989, Charles Handy's seminal book, *The Age of Unreason*, predicted that organizations would contract to the smallest core of full-time workers possible then hire "just in time" workers as needed. His

Nostradamus-like forecast correctly spotted the now commonplace corporate strategy of reducing labor costs whenever such a move serves the interest of the core corporate leadership.

When I was growing up in the 1980s, lay-offs were uncommon and those who were laid off often felt stigmatized. Indeed, one of my most haunting memories was a classmate's father's suicide. By all accounts, when he had a job, he appeared to be a well-adjusted person. But he felt shamed by his long-term unemployment—which was only nine months—and became despondent.

In his 2005 book, *The World Is Flat*, Thomas Friedman described the new interconnectedness of the global economy as having both fantastic and frightening possibilities: Worldwide business opportunities also brought worldwide labor eager to work for little pay. You could sell goods to the giant markets of China and India but eager and talented workers in such places could also do your work at a fraction of the cost.

The Great Recession exacerbated all the negative aspects of these macroeconomic changes. There were far more jobs outsourced than new business opportunities created; far more jobs killed by technology than birthed; and far more secure jobs cut than opportunities generated by self-selected freelancers.

This is not about technological change but rather work structure change

Almost everyone who first heard about the Internet and e-mail in the late twentieth century was oblivious to the onslaught of how the work world would change because of the Information Age revolution. For those who thought that something profound was happening, the focus was upon technological advancement. For information junkies and efficiency fanatics, the changes were embraced: "I can read about anything!" or "I can write something that my friends and co-workers can read in real time!" Few thought, "This means computer algorithms will destroy our industry."

Similarly, nineteenth-century farmers may have looked at the advances of technology with either curiosity or disdain but few would have thought that their way of working would be forever changed. Most were shocked that working their century-old farm would not be a possible career path for their children.

Most parents today are in the same position as those parent-farmers. Whatever label historians agree upon - the Information or Internet or Computer Revolution - has changed the way work has been organized. Mini-revolutions such as globalization, automation, the rise of artificial intelligence and so forth have and will continue to accelerate structural shifts in how work is structured. For many, gone are the days of full-time jobs with benefits into the indefinite future on a distinct and life-long career path, most likely with large organizations

Explaining to parents that finding internships as early as freshman year of college is becoming more common; that the gig economy means that having multiple streams of income makes sense; that some companies will have a "try-out" period; and that switching careers for this generation will be as common as switching jobs was for ours is often met with puzzled expressions, even among my generally highly educated clientele.

Much of the current work world is structured differently than the prior generation's work world. Is this good or bad news? It depends. This can be wonderful. For those who want to work virtually and are able to do so, the option is life changing. This can be terrible. With lifetime employment no longer part of our social construct, companies no longer run the risk of developing a bad reputation for laying off experienced, loyal workers. This can be neutral. From a company's perspective, independent contractors make more fiscal sense than full-time employees. But this also could enable the skilled worker to contract with multiple employers ("clients") to minimize risk.

There will be good and bad. Regardless, parents have to deal with the new reality. Unless your own experiences have schooled you in the way the world of work now operates, realize that some part of the way you understood careers has radically changed.

Perhaps most significantly, and the impetus for many readers to get this book, is that the college to career transition is no longer the sure thing it seemed to be. The reasons for the change are numerous but here are a few:

(1) Proportionally far fewer career building jobs

Let me define career building jobs as work that provides skills, experience, and credentials for financial independence in the present and that should lead to greater, or at least the same, economic rewards in the future. This definition is not designed to diminish restaurant or retail jobs. But unless such jobs are part of a career building plan, they are not within my definition.

Career building jobs for college grads are no longer in proportion to the large number of college graduates. Prior to the Great Recession of 2007-2008, the unemployed or underemployed twentysomething college graduate was a cautionary tale. "I heard Andy still doesn't have a job…"

The dizzying array of macroeconomic factors such as fierce, world-wide, inexpensive competition for "white collar jobs", the change in the basic nature of the employer-employee relationship, automation, artificial intelligence, and other disruptive technologies, and the financial meltdown has created a new reality. Getting a career building job out of college is a serious challenge.

This is, far and away, the biggest reason for the failure to launch phenomenon.

(2) Fewer career training programs at large organizations

Career development and training programs still exist at large organizations but to a much smaller proportional degree. There are far more college graduates for such training programs than spots exist. Moreover, the old sports adage of taking the "best available athlete" was the metaphor for many organizations who hired college graduates without any relevant work or often even academic experience related to the job. The organization would train many entry level workers and, even better, would have rotational programs through different departments. Such programs provided outstanding career exploration.

Today, soon to graduate college students often need internships to get hired since many organizations expect even their entry-level employees to have relevant experience.

(3) Change in employment structures

Employment structures for those new to the workforce has changed. Internships, part-time work, and full-time independent contract work are methods where employers can test—and discard—entry-level workers much more easily. The first job, a generation ago, was envisioned as a multi-year commitment on both ends. Now, the first job is often a multi-month or longer try out.

(4) Flexible work force valued over long term employees

Economic changes are taking place at a breathtaking pace. This makes the commitment to hire someone full time into the indefinite future more problematic. For example, small businesses have to be more cautious in hiring because the skills required today might not be needed tomorrow. Large organizations have to be careful because firing someone in today's litigious atmosphere can be a burdensome proposition. It makes more sense in today's world for many employers to value flexible work relationships over long term committed ones.

(5) A Vast Number of Options In General and a Vast Number of Different options

In simple sum, too many choices leave people immersed in analysis paralysis. Career confusion was—and is—not a challenge for those born into situations with minimal options.

. . . .

MAIN TAKEAWAY:
We are living in a work revolution. Educate yourself accordingly.

LESSON 3:

CALLING DR. FREUD: YOU HAVE TO BE AN AMATEUR PSYCHOLOGIST

THROUGH THE YEARS, COUNTLESS PARENT-CLIENTS HAVE called to express appreciation about getting their twentysomethings "unstuck." As most of us realize when we progress through life, knowing how to do something and having the psychological readiness to do it are different things.

Telling someone to write e-mail inquiries to potential employers is part of the work of career counseling. It is also something that most parents who would take the time to read this book would do. Teaching someone how to write an effective e-mail inquiry is a skill that career counselors have but is also something that many well-educated parents can do as well. Getting someone to write e-mail inquiries seems to be where career *counselors* have a distinct advantage because they are not the parents and, those that are skillful, understand how to navigate the psychological challenges faced by twentysomethings.

Here are some common challenges:

The Perils of Choice

I find the story of mankind fascinating and, of late, am particularly interested in the everyday lives of people from years ago. History, as taught in school, covers the great events and famous people extensively. The lives of the ordinary are skimmed over or are far in the background. We know of Julius Caesar but other than a sense that there were a lot of soldiers and slaves, most know little about the lives of everyday Romans. In relation to career choice, most Romans– even the noblemen—had almost no career choice. The vast majority on the lower end of the socioeconomic ladder—laborers and slaves - were essentially locked into their station for life. The merchants and tradesmen could hope to move within the middle-class strata but were not making their way into the aristocracy by creating the next tech start-up. Most simply followed their parents' footsteps. That pattern dominated not only historically but cross-culturally until the twentieth century and still only in economically mobile societies. Indeed, the American experiment emanated largely from the desire for upward mobility and empowering freedom to "pursue happiness", which included career choice.

Today, twentysomethings in the New World of Work have a vast array of careers to consider. That gift is also a challenge for many career seekers. This was not the case only a few generations ago. Taking over the family store or learning your parent's craft was the presumed singular path for those in such situations. That may sound dim to many. Variety is generally a good thing. Career choice variety, however, can also be headache inducing. Our freedom to choose, while brilliant in theory, has also created enormous challenges. As Barry Schwartz pointed out in *The Paradox of Choice*, vast possibilities create their own set of problems.

Nancy, a recent college graduate, came in for a career counseling session as she was suffering from complete information overload. She had studied nearly a dozen different career paths. She noted the advantages and disadvantages of each and how each could or might not be suited to different parts of her personality.

As expected, her parents told her repeatedly, "You can do whatever you want with your career." I don't discourage parents from conveying this thought to young children. Nonetheless, when young adults tell me that they are lost in part because of seemingly endless career possibilities, I know that the open-ended nature of choice is part of the problem.

This is also a large problem because the "answers" cannot be figured out with certainty. You can't sit down with a pen and paper and figure out with mathematical exactitude which career path is best. Analytical intelligence can get someone only so far in a framework that lacks certainty.

Strategy: Option Analysis

As a parent, how you can help? Children think they can simultaneously become Oscar-winning actors and Olympic gymnasts. No need to disillusion them. But twentysomethings need a reality check.

While I do not relish bursting bubbles, I do go through an option analysis exercise that provides clarity. What are your real options? Let's go through each. This exercise provides surprising clarity. Twentysomethings routinely tell me that they are confused by "so many choices". Even though the choices are far more than our ancestors, they have far fewer choices than they think. Quite often, their career choices are not so much about concrete jobs or career paths but rather desires. For example, many are conflicted about pursuing a path of passion, which often correlates with risk versus more secure paths. But the conflict is often abstract. I'll ask, "What is the passion that you want to pursue?" "I don't really know" is the most common response. I rarely hear, "I want to pursue a singing career." Instead, I usually hear themes like "I want to love my work" or "I want to be really rich." Either way, so be it, but I tell my clients, as you should your children, "let's list the actual career paths given your current situation that have the best chance of leading to your goals."

Similarly, when I am working with clients who are comparing more standard options, let's say sales versus marketing, I show them "this is it", as in right now, these are the two general paths. There are not hundreds of options. This sometimes is disheartening but often clarity provides power.

"It Will Come to Me"

Our K-college programming created false programming regarding how transitions occur. "Change"—sometimes massive change like heading to college—happened to us automatically. We proceeded from grade to grade through an outside process. College choice was the first major decision for most young adults and explains, in part, why the process is so stressful. For example, those who went through the process of choosing boarding schools are almost always less stressed about college decisions because they made a significant life decision before. Regardless, college choice has a forced timeline and a clear-cut process.

Career choice is not analogous. There are no application deadlines or Common Application. The thought that the end of college would be that time and that a college education would be that process was an illusion. There exists a pervasive cultural myth that sometime during high school or college we would figure out what work we wanted to do for the rest of our lives. How this actually happens is never quite explained.

At most, young adults are told that they will take classes in something they like that will lead to natural gravitation toward a specific career. The mismatch between high-school classes and real-world careers, while never particularly correlative, has grown increasingly wider. As for college, the challenges facing liberal-arts students choosing careers are now well known. I loved my philosophy, theology, psychology, English, government, and history classes. The education itself was enlightening, enriching, and stimulating. Indeed, the Great Books are often source material for developing intrapersonal wisdom which leads to happier personal and professional lives. I struggle to say anything negative about a liberal-arts education. However, the course work provided minimal career insight.

As for business students, most are doing course work that more closely provides exposure to career choice. Nevertheless, there are radical variations in business careers. Creating Excel spreadsheets from reams of statistical data is a business job, but so is creating a multimedia marketing campaign.

Engineers, premeds, and others in technical fields are far closer to getting simultaneous academic and career training. The problem is that the course work itself does not compel students to sort out big-picture career questions. The eighteen-year-old college freshman who chose her specialist technical path correctly has good fortune. Those who chose incorrectly become unhappy thirtysomething health care practitioners and computer programmers.

Many of my twentysomething clients seem to think that career answers will magically come to them. Since that does not happen for most, I have to instill a process.

Strategy: Regular time for Exploratory Work

Perhaps the biggest missing piece of our educational system is our lack of career exploratory work. Our College to Career Program will be described more distinctly in the next part of the book. But here is a snippet that describes part of the process.

I suggest that young adults start examining companies, organizations and jobs within each that might interest them. So, for example, the business world—where most jobs are located—is a mystery to most high school students and still mostly a mystery to many college students. Reading magazines and newspapers—presumably online—such as the traditional *Fortune, Forbes*, and the *Wall St. Journal* and the more modern, such as *Fast Company, Inc., and Entrepreneur,* with the simple directive: find what interests you.

Michael was a highly confused twenty-year-old who was terrified about the world of work because he had no exposure to anything that interested him. His father was a physician. His mother was a stay at home mom. Their family friends were mostly in health care. He had no interest in anything medical. He began the reading-research-reflection part of our College to Career Program and quickly found himself loving the start-up culture. He wasn't exactly sure which industry attracted him the most but he thought the idea of being on the ground floor of a company would be exciting and would suit his generalist skill set. He had a sense that he would wind up in marketing or sales but he liked the idea that he could contribute to different operational areas as tends to be required in the start-up phases of companies. We had worked together in the summer. When he went back to school, he joined his college's entrepreneur club, secured an internship at a Boston based start-up, and wrote me at the end of the summer that he was staying in Boston as he a landed a summer job at a different Boston start-up.

Analysis Paralysis and Dealing with Ambiguity

Analysis paralysis blocks people from moving forward: those frozen in career blocks are often stuck because of process and outcome ambiguity. I am not referring to the feeling of being lost, having no idea what to do is different than knowing the right direction but being unable to move forward. Some of our clients cannot move forward because they do not know how to move forward (process ambiguity) and/or because the results of moving forward are not guaranteed (outcome ambiguity).

Process Ambiguity

Those who do not know how something works will not move forward even if they know the direction of interest. But most process issues that have practical answers. You might not like some of those answers. Within reason, however, process issues can be sorted out.

Strategy: Workarounds Solve Most Process Issues

Process issues usually have practical solutions that I call workarounds: if you are committed to getting around a tangible problem, there is most often a strategic way around, over, or through the problem or at least a way to deal with the challenge well enough to move forward. Here are some questions that clients typically ask

"I have no idea what graduate or training programs would help me."

"How will I get the money to start a business?"

"I don't know how I will be able to make a career switch."

The first step responses could be:

"Spend a few hours researching graduate or training programs that might suit you."

"You can wait tables while you start your business."

"Find someone who switched fields from your current one to another. Buy her lunch and listen to her story."

Most workarounds are not perfect. Presumably, your child would rather hang out with his friends on Saturday night than wait tables and would feel awkward asking a stranger to tell her story.

Nonetheless, working through ambiguity is the answer. "I don't know how to create a website," Gail said. This was one of ten different objections Gail had with regard to starting a side business. "If I demonstrate that you can build a website, will you then realize that your other objections are equally solvable?" I proposed. As anyone who has used simple site-building software knows, building a basic website is surprisingly easy. Gail was stunned by the simplicity and agreed that she would now look at process challenges differently.

Outcome Ambiguity

Unlike process ambiguity, which has answers for what can be done, outcome ambiguity exists because there are no real answers, just reasonable predictions to "what if" questions.

"What if I don't get admitted?"

"What if I don't get hired?"

"What if the business makes no money?"

Strategy: The Dispassionate Scientist Exercise

Outcome ambiguity cannot be solved like process ambiguity. You can research schools, search for jobs, and start writing a business plan, and each of these activities relieves the anxiety that comes from process ambiguity. The anxiety stemming from outcome ambiguity is fundamentally different because uncertainty about the outcome is the only thing guaranteed as you move forward. The best you can do is remove emotion as you evaluate whether to move forward. Pretend you are a dispassionate scientist hired to consider the odds of your next venture's success.

Over the years, I've worked with thousands of anxious students as they applied to colleges and graduate schools. Some would have rational concerns: "I don't think I'll get into Harvard." Most would have irrational concerns: "I don't think I'll get into Podunk State." With the latter concern, I asked students to step outside themselves and give some percentage chance of admission for a student with the same exact academic profile. Assuming the students made reasonable assessments, they would feel better.

Career issues are more complicated because there is no equivalent of *U.S. News & World Report* data for career outcomes. Nonetheless, if you engage in market analysis, you should be able to make reasonable predictions regarding potential success.

Robert was interested in law school, but news regarding unemployed attorneys worried him. Unquestionably, such news should be part of his evaluation of pursuing law school. Given his high LSAT score and GPA, he was likely to gain admission to a top-twenty law school. The dispassionate scientist would suggest that his data gathering be focused on employment for students from upper-echelon law schools. He discovered that the bulk of unemployed lawyers came from lower-tiered schools. From the perspective of a dispassionate scientist, he better understood his odds, and that propelled him to move forward.

Strategy: Dealing Effectively with Ambiguity is a Valuable Life Skill

Jack DeGioia, the revered long-time president of Georgetown University, was kind enough to provide guidance to me when I was in my twenties. One of his nuggets of wisdom was, "The ability to deal effectively with ambiguity is one of life's most underrated skills." He gave this counsel in relation to one of my career choice points: I had been offered a position as an assistant attorney general for the newly formed nation of Palau, a beautiful island in the South Pacific. Similar to the Marshall Islands, Palau had a protectorate relationship with the United States and thus sought out US government attorneys to help build their legal system. I was bored in my work prosecuting securities violations in Washington, DC, and I initially thought my wife and I could enjoy a couple of years in an idyllic paradise. I would be one of a small group of attorneys prosecuting crimes and representing the government in other high-level matters. Sounded great.

My excitement soon sunk into a morass of ambiguity. If I spent two years off the normal legal track would future employers think this move interesting or flaky (outcome ambiguity)? Palau did not have Internet access at the time, so applying for jobs back in the United States would be very complicated (process ambiguity). I was frozen in analysis paralysis. The decision was ultimately forged by personal considerations—my wife and I wanted to start a family and thought it best to have our first child near our extended family.

I was twenty-eight years old at the time and had not yet adequately developed the skills to deal with ambiguity. Through the decades that followed, I reflected on President DeGioia's advice many times. As a society, we tend not to think of psychological strengths as skills that can be developed, or that such skills have practical application. But neither is true. In *Siddhartha*, Herman Hesse's classic novel inspired by the life of the Buddha, Siddhartha explains one of his skills to a potential employer: "I can wait." Learning to be patient was a skill Siddhartha had cultivated and that proved highly valuable to the merchant who hired him. Similarly, the ability to deal with ambiguity is a skill that should be practiced. Teach your children to be more willing to embrace uncertainty. Not only will the ability to deal effectively with ambiguity decrease their anxiety levels, but it will also enable them to take calculated risks for career advancement.

"I Want It All."

Sydney was a 22-year-old graduate from an elite college. She had two distinct goals: (1) she wanted to work for international non-profits located in Africa and (2) she wanted to be a young and highly involved mother. To that end, she and her serious boyfriend had discussed getting married and starting a family in their early twenties. I would imagine that most mothers reading Sydney's goals just laughed.

"What do you want from your career?" is a common career-counseling question, and "I want it all," is a common response, particularly from idealists. My counsel: you might be waiting for a perfect spouse or career but this can only cause problems when searching for either.

I often listen to desires that create an immediate sense of improbability:

"I want to earn a lot of money, and I don't want a demanding job."

"I want to be my own boss, and I want security."

"I want to be a constant presence for my children, and I want to travel for work."

I then provide another tool that helps my clients.

Strategy: Use the Must-Want Continuum to Prioritize

Each career field has its bumps. To sort out which bumps matter, I make my clients evaluate their options through a "Must-Want Continuum." I created this paradigm after hearing clients list their desires without any prioritization and without recognizing that many of their desires conflicted with how things play out in the real world. Those highly paid/low-pressure jobs are not plentiful. Younger clients, in particular, will list their career demands, then cross off possibilities if one of those demands is not met.

I make my clients place their career desires along a continuum with Must on one end and Want (as in nice to have but not essential) on the other end. Prioritization does wonders to burst magical thinking. Separating the essential from the added benefit, but not highly important, will help evaluate possibilities. If a client places high income far closer to Must than low pressure, then she can see what really matters to her. If your main goal is to maximize income, then you likely will be dealing with some pressure, and that's fine if low pressure provides only a small benefit. Similarly, those who tell me they want to have a full-time job, but want the freedom to work from home will need to categorize which is more important, as will those who want the autonomy of entrepreneurship and the relative security of organizational employment.

Strategy: Understand That You Might Be Able to Have It All, Just Not All at Once

I also show clients that while it is possible to have it all, having it all at once is usually challenging. Jobs with extensive world travel usually do not mix well with those who also want to be highly involved parents.

Indeed, getting the adventure bug out in one's twenties before settling down in one's thirties is a common paradigm. The area where I live presents an idyllic coastal life. Many of my clients say they would like to live here but vibrant social scenes for twentysomethings are more prevalent in cities. As with many life choices, our clients have to select which priority is dominant at their current stage of life.

Fear Is the Foundational Block

Fear underlies all of the preceding psychological blocks, and it deserves its own section. What are your children most afraid of? Public failure? Lack of security? Being wrong? Disappointing themselves? Losing control? These psychological issues are often repressed but must be confronted.

Financial Failure

For many, the basic career fear centers upon money. Some fears, however, are irrational or at least overstated. In response to questions about not moving forward with their dream careers, some young clients respond: "I might starve or become homeless." Even if my clients are conveying only the figurative possibility that they may become unable to afford basic necessities, I tell them to stop being irrational.

My view comes from a place of deep gratitude, not entitlement. Readers of this book most likely have extraordinary good fortune. If we lived during most every other historical era or in many places of the world today, both starvation and homelessness could become a reality for those unable to earn money for an extended period of time.

That your child has the luxury of pondering career choice likely places them in fortunate enough circumstances that they have family, friends, and acquaintances who would help them if they were in dire straits, and multiple public and private safety nets that would further serve to buffer any fall. They will not starve, and it is highly unlikely that they will become homeless.

Strategy: Separating the Rational from the Irrational

The first step to combat generalized fear is to separate rational from irrational fears. Confront the rational ones by evaluating the real downside and plan accordingly. As for the irrational fears, dealing with anxiety is complicated. I tell my clients who are angst-ridden when contemplating career questions to role-play being a monk or a robot confronting similar issues. Strange, I know. But those who are advanced spiritually and those who are exclusively rational do not suffer anxiety. They simply deal with the challenges peacefully and rationally. Embracing Stoic philosophy is the other best strategy: Focus only on what you can control.

For most twentysomethings, rational fear is financial instability, not starvation. Analytically evaluate how certain career moves will impact their finances. With these facts in mind, they can make rational decisions about risk rather than grappling with imagined monsters under the bed.

Public Failure

"When you're 20 you care what everybody thinks, when you're 40 you stop caring what everyone thinks, when you're 60, you realize no one was ever thinking about you in the first place."

– Winston Churchill

Many of my young clients are afraid of failure because they worry about what others will think. I understand that fear all too well. In my younger years, I worried about what "they" would think. As I became more self-aware, I asked myself who "they" are and found that I did not know and did not really care.

I realized that if I failed, those who genuinely cared for me would still do so. People one step out of my circle of real friends and family were the "they," an undefined audience of people who were not really watching me. This part of "they" would barely give a moment's thought about my fortunes. Why? "They" are fully consumed with their own lives because of self-absorption and/or healthy attunement to what really matters to them. "They" don't care about my career or yours, I tell my young clients.

To illustrate this point, I tell them to spend a few moments watching the audience the next time at any children's theatre or musical performance. Parents are singularly focused upon their own children, barely noticing anyone else's. The same concept holds true in relation to the career paths of others.

Strategy: Reevaluate How Much "They" Think about You

If your children are not moving forward with a potentially great career plan because they fear negative public perception if they flounder, suggest they reevaluate their perception of how much others spend time thinking about them. If they think it will be embarrassing to strive for a goal and fail because "everyone" will know and everyone will care, then they should realize that few will know and even fewer will care, at least in a negative way.

Those who do hear of their problems—and care about them—will wish them well and offer to help. Those who do not like them, or feel in competition with them, may have their moment of Schadenfreude, but your children will never know. Moreover, they might seem more likable to such envious types who are more likely to kick them when they are up than when they are down. And as anyone who has lived long enough to develop a modicum of wisdom knows, life is too short to worry about what those you don't respect think.

Personal Failure

Your children might be their own toughest audience. Perfectionists have this issue. No one likes being wrong. But some people are overly self-critical, which makes being wrong particularly terrible for them. Taking a risk by definition means one might get it wrong. Your task is to get your children to treat themselves better if things don't go well.

Jessica had spent the last decade dreaming about opening a yoga studio. A meticulous planner, Jessica had the financing, location, teachers, and client base—she just had to take the leap. "But what if I do something wrong and it fails?" Jessica's practical downside was not too bad: she could go back to teaching at other yoga institutes, she was not too bothered by public perception, and her peer group and family were supportive.

But Jessica was her own toughest critic. "I'll beat myself up over everything that goes wrong." She says. Even if the venture didn't fail, Jessica worried that she would constantly berate herself for the inevitable mistakes that come with starting a business.

"You'll be tough to work for," I said, knowing this was not true, as Jessica was very kindhearted.

"What do you mean?" Jessica asked.

"When your staff makes mistakes, you will be really tough on them."

"No, I'm not like that with others."

We then discussed what I already knew: Jessica treated others far better than she treated herself. She agreed that she treated others well not only because she wanted to be nice, but because doing so was also more effective. She then understood the point: being self-critical was not serving her.

Strategy: Apply the Golden Rule to Oneself

Are your children worried about disappointing themselves? Teach them to learn to treat themselves as they would treat others. As children, most perfectionists created internal programming along the lines of "If I'm tough on myself, I will get it right." At some point, such criticism isn't necessary for success.

LESSON 4:

WE ARE ALL CONSULTANTS OR TV ACTORS OR ENTREPRENEURS

THE STRANGEST "THING TO DO" IS CHANGING THE MINDSET OF your children from that of employees to that of consultants. Or TV actors. Or entrepreneurs. Many of your children will not have full-time jobs, with benefits, into the indefinite future, on distinct life-long career paths for large organizations. They might strive to do so, particularly when starting out and they may find such jobs for stretches of time. But most will not.

What does each of these labels mean?

We are all Consultants

In the 1990s movie *Father of the Bride*, Steve Martin's character skeptically questions his daughter's fiancée about his career when she notes that he is "a consultant." "Doesn't that mean you are unemployed or can't keep a job?" It turns out that the fiancée is in such demand due to his skills that companies can't afford to retain him full time. Given his place in the marketplace, he can choose what projects interest him, earn more money than if he had a single job, and work less time than he would if was an employee. That's the type of invincibility that we all should strive to attain.

I was recently working with a 26-year-old client in the big data field. Working for a large organization, he was treated well. His compensation was solid. His boss and co-workers were nice enough. Even though he was working in Manhattan, he was not overworked. But, after reading my earlier work *Career Path of Abundance* in which I described that the path of greatest happiness often lies within an entrepreneurial endeavor, he thought that he would be happier, and likely more successful, going out on his own. He devised a plan and then came to see me. I did not do much other than give him the green light after we tweaked his plans. He affirmatively chose to become a consultant. That doesn't mean he'll never go back to the big firm life. He simply recognizes that he can attain greater success on his own.

Or TV Actors

I have a wonderfully talented old friend who works primarily on visual effects for TV shows. He has worked on pilots that did not go anywhere and on several multi-year shows. And, he also has chosen, occasionally, to take himself off the job market to create his own stuff. At the time of this writing, he is working for a major TV show but, knowing him and also the reality of show business, I imagine he'll be onto a new adventure soon enough. His career path will resemble the majority of career paths in the future.

Think about how jobs in the television industry come about. TV shows start with pilots. The pilots are either bought or rejected by TV networks. More shows are purchased based on the network's prediction of the show's success. Some shows seemingly run forever—*60 Minutes, The Simpsons, The Today Show*—some run as long as the creators wish—*Seinfeld, The Sopranos, Breaking Bad*—some go for a few years and many disappear or never get aired at all. These shows are all little businesses that employ dozens to hundreds of people. Each worker has a peripatetic career. Those with their careers in the movie industry, not just actors but the thousands of behind-the-scenes workers who bring movies to life, have even more drastic non-linear careers.

Our children's careers, presumably most outside of Hollywood, will have a similar feel.

Or Entrepreneurs

This Information Age Revolution has led to massive creative freedom. I tell our young clients: If you have a business idea and a few hundred dollars, you could start a multi-national company today. Open your computer. Create a website with the relatively simple do it yourself web building software; a transactional link to your bank account so consumers can buy whatever it is you are selling; if needed, hire independent contractors who live across the globe through a reputable freelancer site and…. you now have a multi-national company.

The work revolution has opened entrepreneurial possibilities for most anyone. This is extraordinarily great news for our children who are suited for entrepreneurialism. No more waiting in line for a promotion. No more bosses. Get to The American Dream quickly. Moreover, status worries are often as much of a challenge as financial worries for the unemployed. Fortunately, today, "I'm starting a company" or "I'm working on a company started by a friend" is now a perfectly respectable story.

. . . .

MAIN TAKEAWAY:

The old employer-employee relationship is over.
Embrace the new freedom that comes from
consulting and/or building businesses.

LESSON 5:

UNDERSTAND WHY THE NEW GENERATION HAS TO WORK BOTH INSIDE AND OUTSIDE THE GRID

Inside the Grid: The old paradigm of the straight linear path

In the 20th century college to career transition paradigm, most college seniors sought and gained employment from large organizations. Many stayed in large organizations for the bulk of their careers. The Organization Man, as such types were commonly called, followed the conventional successful path. These types work **"inside the grid"**, my term for staying within the organization framework and not venturing out on their own.

For most, working inside the grid was better than attempting to forge one's unique path. The large organizational framework continued the clear and straight path for many achievers: K-12, college, maybe graduate school, and then life-long employment climbing the corporate ladder. The same paradigm also provided clarity for the more easy-going type: gain entry to a large organization—even in a low-level white-collar job—get a modest but predictable raise each year and hang on long enough to get a pension.

Outside the Grid: The new paradigm of the sometimes straight, sometimes multiple, sometimes nonexistent path.

When my father retired in the early 2000s, he had already experienced the beginning of the shift. Many of his colleagues were let go during different organizational shake-ups. Most did not realize that the New World of Work was upon us. Life-long employment was about to become a quaint notion.

Not only are organizations no longer the promised land for career development but there are other options that are often more attractive. Small businesses, entrepreneurs, and consultants have always existed. But until the Internet revolution, the vast majority of college seniors did not seek work from such enterprises. Now, many do, either because they have no choice or because they view this path as more promising. We'll label those that do as "**outside the grid.**"

Once someone is not in a large hierarchy, the lines of advancement get blurry and sometimes disappear. Those working for small businesses can get extraordinary and unexpected opportunities without waiting in a long line. The entrepreneur can land a huge life-changing deal—perhaps after years of putting herself in position to land the contract—at a time not governed by corporate promotion policy. The free-lancing consultant might get an opportunity to work in Europe for two years which might change the entire trajectory of his life. And, of course, sudden reversals of fortune could easily occur as well.

But with the right planning, your children can develop invincibility against the macro-economic twists that smash those inside the grid and the mishaps that can pose challenges for those outside the grid.

Living Outside the grid

When I am with people my age, I usually stay silent about my work world. Most are locked into the conventional work world of large organizations. They are immersed in office politicking, title striving, and, budget worrying. They discuss the "fires" they put out or use terms like "battle" and other war-like terms such as "corporate warrior". Even one of my CEO friends tells me that he often wishes he could change jobs with a mailman, believing that he would have a happier, worry-free, day to day lifestyle. I stay quiet because I don't want to create further angst, particularly among those who are likely going to stay in the matrix for the rest of their careers.

But as a parent, you should tell your children that there is another world of work. I was cultured and spent a decade in the traditional confines of large stodgy organizations. Not everything is terrible in such places. Security—even if illusory—is comforting. But, having to put on the facade of the Gray Flannel Man (or woman) every day is soul draining for many.

Those who have spent time in start-ups or other entrepreneurial ventures have a radically different view of work reality. It is not utopia. There are different battles. But, the battles are consequential—"what market should we focus upon?" as opposed to territorial—"I better get placed on the project." Facades are mostly removed. You still need to be nice to the boss but you don't have to put on a phony front for 10 hours a day. The "battles" that you face and the "fires" to put out will be connected to the well-being of the company or your company in ways that you can see. And, while you might work just as much, the good results—such as the company's performance—will likely enhance your life in a more direct way.

Escaping the rat race

Anyone over 40 likely knows the phrase: "Escaping the rat race". It was a pipe dream for many, at least back in the 1980s/1990s. Most thought their work destiny inevitably led to commuting to a large organization, playing the corporate game, and then repeating. Endlessly. Having to deal with face time, organizational politics, rigid schedules, and company policies were/are the bane of career existence for many. This work world—the grid - still exists but, while still a dominant paradigm, is fading.

The desire for greater work-life balance was the first force that led many to reconsider the daily repetitive grind, particularly parents who felt stressed about not spending time with their children. Again, the start-up world of Internet companies led to a different ethos. Those in such companies worked just as hard but rigid schedules became radically less important. Further shifts that accelerated the ability for entrepreneurial ventures of all sorts increased the movement away from the rat race.

I don't want to pretend that those who are untethered from the rat race live in a blissful work world. The challenges of not being in a large organization can be significant. But for those who have success-ful work outside the grid, work life is pretty great. The main reason is greater control of time. For those in demanding jobs in metropolitan areas, eleven-twelve-hour days are standard. Leave the house in the 7-8 am range, commute for thirty minutes to an hour, get to work somewhere in the 8-9 range, leave work in the 6-7 range and arrive home in the 7-8 pm range.

For those outside of large organizations, the amount of actual work time might be the same. But face time potentially disappears. No need to make sure to stay just because the boss will notice your absence. I recall leaving my law office to a court hearing that was near my house. I finished around 1 pm. Driving back to work would have taken another hour. So, I decided to work at home as there were no meetings or anything else requiring in-person interaction back at the office. The law partner's irritated response: "if we have to be here, so do you." Commuting—if needed at all—usually can be done in off traffic hours.

My recent work with a whole host of clients who have moved to a self-created work world may ultimately prove to be my most fulfilling work. They report that not only did our career counseling program change their work lives but dramatically changed their overall happiness and well-being.

Those that choose to work outside the grid have likely embraced a cultural shift for some: large organizations create corporate drones, not pillars of society. The truth is somewhere in-between and, as always, idiosyncratic preference is all that matters. Regardless, even those who prefer the security—or at least feelings of security that large organizations engender—will be forced to make money at various times in their career outside large organizations.

My own path reflects this transition. I started my career staying within the lines. College-law school-large legal organizations. Then, in the year 2000, I strayed from the linear path and went the entrepreneurial route. That move made all the difference in my career. When I first left, the most common question from my lawyer brethren and others in large organizations was "why?" As time passed, most increasingly and, now almost exclusively, ask "how?"

The soon to be invincible recent college graduate

A few years ago, I was approached by a young entrepreneur, Simon, who had recently graduated from Yale with multiple honors. He and his team had created a product that would streamline the backend operations of education companies. He came to pitch me his company's services. We drifted into a good conversation about his path. When I graduated in the late 1980s, talented achievers primarily went into medicine, law, and investment banking. They still do, of course, but some choose to take the non-traditional route. When I asked Simon about his choice, he responded that "sure, I could go the normal route. But that's a bit boring, like if you can't think of anything else to do. I want to create my own thing."

If you can play within a system and create your own system, you will be invincible

Michael Jordan, Reggie Miller, and Earl Magnigut. Every reader knows Jordan, basketball fans recognize Miller, but only the most ardent basketball fans have heard of Magnigut. Jordan was great for many reasons. For the career metaphor, we'll focus on his ability to create his own shot at any time while also scoring at will within the famed triangle offensive system. He was great within and without a system. That made him invincible.

Miller was among the greatest pure shooters in NBA history. But he needed teammates to set picks and pass to him when he was positioned to shoot. Miller could play well within a team construct that enabled his success. But he had limited ability to score outside of a team system that was designed to support him.

As for Magnignut, he was a phenomenal talent in the freewheeling playgrounds of New York City. If you ever wondered who was the first person to get the moniker "the GOAT" as in Greatest of All Time, many think it was Earl "The GOAT" Magnignut. But he could only play on the outside of a professional team system, both figuratively due to his individual playing style, and literally, as he never made the NBA due, in part, to his lifestyle choices.

Regarding that aforementioned Yale entrepreneur, by learning how to create his own business he had almost definitely set himself up for success. He was discovering how to create his own shot. If his venture failed, he could go back and work on the inside—the benefits of Yale help in this regard—or he could sharpen his approach and try again to score on his own.

Those who can figure out how to be valuable within the organizational grid and without will be invincible. Others will need to figure out where they best belong: in or out of the grid.

. . . .

MAIN TAKEAWAY:
Skills, not large organizations, provide security.
Teach your children to be able to work both within
and outside of organizations,

LESSON 6:

ALWAYS BE BUILDING

IN HOMAGE TO *GLENGARRYGLENROSS'S* FAMOUS "ALWAYS BE Closing" speech, I often suggest that clients "always be building." It is highly likely that your children: (1) will face periods of unemployment (2) change career paths (3) change organizations routinely and (4) need to develop new skills to earn money.

The increased need to "be ready" for the next career, job, or gig may be the biggest shift in the history of work. This is not hyperbolic. Lifetime jobs of farmers, manual laborers, merchants and other prevalent career paths of the past were static. Those in such jobs had no need to upgrade their skills, dust off their resumes to job search, or read about new developments that would affect their industries. Similarly, the steady job paradigm of the twentieth-century kept workers in place for years. This generation will need to embrace constant change.

Relying on someone else for a paycheck has become far riskier than in the past. Having the ability to create your own money is the best way to mitigate that risk. How this done is as much a mindset as a process. Those ensconced in corporate thinking rarely consider the possibility of creating something outside of their organization.

Here's what your children should do or, at least consider, regardless of their current work situation:

(1)   Build a side business

(2)   Have a plan to get or actually get a part-time job

(3)   Continually engage in exploratory work

(4)   Save money as a "war chest" for inevitable transitions

(5)   Continually develop marketable skills

The Side Business

I advise many of our career counseling clients that they should consider creating a side business. Here's why:

(1) Hedge Against Unemployment

Unfortunately, the new employer-employee contract is so tenuous that your children could be terminated from their current jobs at any time. If they have a side business, then they have a ready-made "fill the gap" on their resumes. In addition, while it is unlikely that their side business will replace their full-time job's income in the short term, at least they will have some income. Thereafter, they might be able to build the business to match their prior income.

(2) Stress reduction

Whatever stresses their full-time job creates, they will know that they potentially have the option to build out their business. Even if they stay in their job, the thought that they have an option to leave will help get them through tough days. Does this matter? Absolutely. Feeling trapped is among the top reasons I hear from career counseling clients who are miserable in their current jobs.

(3) They might end up creating a great business or an alternative to working for someone else

Many great companies started as side businesses. But we don't have to get ahead of ourselves. What if they simply could create a business that matches their current income? That would give them a delightful positive dilemma.

(4) Multiple streams of income

Many readers are likely familiar with the term and perhaps more readily consider investments as opposed to jobs within this framework. Given the precarious nature of the New World of Work, having 100% of one's income from a single source is not advisable. Regardless, it is my general career counseling view that in the New World of Work, we all need to be more entrepreneurial. Starting their own side business is the safest way to educate themselves on how to do so.

In Silicon Valley and other tech hub spots, many full-time employees simultaneously work on outside business ventures with their friends. This may seem to be a path only for the highly ambitious. But it now makes sense for not only those who want to create the next killer app but for most anyone.

Ideally, the side business should be within their field of career expertise or at least in whatever area they hope to develop for their next career stage. The corporate accountant who does personal tax work or the web designer of a large corporation who does web marketing for small businesses are examples. Or it could be something entirely different such as the office manager who starts a side business selling rare dolls on eBay.

Planning for or having a part-time job:

Except for the possibility of creating a business, a part-time job has all the benefits listed above. Indeed, whenever I counsel would-be entrepreneurs, I ask some variation of "are you willing to wait tables (or bartend or work retail)?" My question is designed to test the commitment the entrepreneur has to the venture. Actors understand this model well. If they are going to make a career of acting, they know there will be many days between paydays. They need a part-time job. Knowing full well the busyness of a full-time job, it might not be realistic to have a full time and part time job. Being in position to have one is the next best thing. For example, one of my clients, Peter, was an electronic gadget enthusiast. For fun, he would browse new items at electronics stores. During his plan for career transition, he suffered over figuring out ways to pay his bills if he ultimately made the leap to his new career path. I suggested that he work part-time at a local store that he frequented. The manager—who knew Peter from his many visits - needed part-time help during the holiday season. Not only did Peter enjoy his new gig, while making some extra money, but he felt entirely empowered. He realized that there were ways to make money outside the trappings of his current employer. Assuming they do not violate any moonlighting or non-compete clauses, having, or being in a position to quickly obtain, a part-time job will be empowering.

Even if your adult children are fully employed and in no need of a part-time job, the mere exercise of having a plan in place should their income disappear will be comforting whether it is being able to provide some part-time help to a small business or working retail it will ease their mind and potentially stave off financial disaster.

Career exploration—the no (or minimal) risk way of seeking to live a better life

"I realized that I'm settling for a steady but dreary work life," Morgan said in our introductory phone call. Morgan was in the real estate field in New London, Connecticut. "I have no reason to quit. The pay is ok. My boss is ok. My work is ok. My lifestyle is ok. Compared to a lot of others, I have it pretty good."

I liked Morgan's attitude of gratitude. Even if you don't like your job, starting in a place of gratitude for having a job that, at least, pays the bills is a good thing from both a spiritual/psychological place and from a practical place because it is easier to move when infused with positive energy.

"I just don't want to risk switching careers." Morgan continued. I explained to Morgan that she wasn't risking anything at the moment. She was not near the point of making a leap. But, she was engaged in a process that stops many people from exploring their dreams. She was comparing her current job with a phantom job. Certainty beats uncertainty almost every time.

What is the risk of career exploration? Reading/reflecting/discussing work in other fields with friends/acquaintances. That costs nothing and the time invested is hardly a cost. Taking a class might cost some money but the whole notion of stopping education after college is rapidly becoming outdated. Meeting with a skilled career counselor—warning self-serving notice—is potentially life-changing and, at worst, an hour with an objective advisor who might provide a few insights for the cost of dinner at a nice restaurant. Regardless, how big of a risk is that in the context of something as significant as your career?

Career exploration is risk-free. Staying in a job or career path that you don't like is risk-free only if you think being mildly unhappy for the rest of your working days is worth the price of certainty.

Save for the transition war chest

You likely have preached the benefits of saving. Saving for transition is now one more important basket to go with a first house and a starter retirement plan. Transitions will be inevitable for most. Having worked with dozens of clients who were let go with minimal warning and minimal savings as well as those who affirmatively were planning a switch, I cannot emphasize enough the psychological and practical difference a savings fund designed for this specific reason mattered. I fully realize that this is difficult. But I know with certainty who will foot the bill for most young adults if they have no transition fund—their parents

Instruct your children on the new lesson of money management: you are your unemployment insurance and you are your venture capital fund. In relation to unemployment, tell them they might be lucky to either get severance or unemployment but even those benefits only go so far. In relation to starting their own ventures, there is only one source of certain funding: them.

Continually Develop Marketable Skills

The ability to learn most anything through self-education has to be among the highest benefits of the Information Age. Formal credentials certainly matter but those that can demonstrate knowledge and skills for jobs can compete with others, even without degrees. For example, there are several websites with cheap or inexpensive lessons in coding. Understanding computer languages, if only to communicate with the technically skilled, will be a vital skill in the twenty-first century.

When I am asked about my own transformation from someone with a liberal arts education to attorney with mostly public service experience to education-entrepreneur, I note that the "moment" I had made the change was built upon hundreds of hours reading about all the facets of entrepreneurship. Moreover, the biggest boost in growing The Learning Consultants stemmed from my self-education about search engine optimization, a technical skill that had nothing to do with my formal education.

· · · · · · · · ·

MAIN TAKEAWAY:
Always be building your career and there are many ways do to so.

LESSON 7:

HOW TO BE A GUIDE:

HOW TO HELP IS A MUCH BIGGER, MORE NUANCED TOPIC. THE contours of your relationship with your children are so unique that general suggestions will likely not be of much use. Here, I know outsiders—such as career counselors - have a big advantage over parents. Part of our company's success has stemmed from giving advice that parents would have given or have given but that young adults simply tuned out because the advice was coming from their parents. Counselors or other trusted advisors are a default if your relationship would prevent effective consultation with your client.

Nonetheless, I can tell you what I have found effective.

(1) Choosing the time and place for discussions

Barking at your child when he is watching TV or playing on his phone: "you should get a job..." will not help. Selecting a time that is *convenient for your child* will set the stage for a productive conversation.

The best way to do so is through scheduling. "I want to schedule a time where I can discuss how I can help you…." As for the place, somewhere that is free from distractions is best. I find walking to be ideal for big picture discussions.

(2) Ensuring that your state is calm

Your stress about your child's situation will prevent a healthy conversation. When you are stressed, it will be the worst time for a discussion. Your energy will be picked up by your child and things will deteriorate quickly from that point forward. I cannot emphasize this point enough: only talk about your adult child's career issues when you are in a peaceful state of mind.

(3) Lead with "I'm here to help, not judge or boss"

Starting with "I'm here to help you. I realize that you are putting pressure on yourself. My role is to assist you as best I can", will go a long way to beginning the conversation in a positive way. The challenge with the parent-advisor is the highly complicated transition from unconditional nurturer (young child) to boss-nag (teen years) to mentor-guide (adulthood). Expressly noting that you are not having the conversation to either evaluate or order them will help the shift.

(4) Be clear on your goals for the conversation

Your child will not have a job at the end of a conversation with you. Leading the conversation by presenting a list of job openings will likely create stress. Your goal might simply be to open up the conversational pathway or to listen or to provide emotional support. Thereafter, if you can work effectively with your child, then helping find jobs or craft cover letters may be the next practical step.

(5) Recognize the emotional challenge

"How are you feeling?" even if acknowledged with a grunt is a possible way to start a potentially stressed conversation. Letting your child vent helps as does simply acknowledging that you know they are not happy about their situation either.

(6) Lead with open-ended questions

I started my career as a criminal prosecutor. We were quickly trained in the art of examining witnesses. As all trial lawyers know, open-ended questions such as the proverbial "what happened on the night of…?" are best for eliciting long responses. We would ask our witnesses questions that would allow them the chance to elaborate. Cross-examination, by contrast, tries to lock opposing witnesses into statements that help your side. "Isn't it true that…?" Parents tend to ask such questions: "did you contact Mr. Rutledge about his firm?" The "no" answer immediately creates tension.

If you find yourself asking yes/no questions, immediately change your tactics. Your children won't like cross-examination any more than opposing witnesses do from trial attorneys.

(7) Listen as much as possible

Lectures will be tuned out as will repetition. "Tell me… [what's on your mind?] [your concerns] [your hopes] [what's the plan?] [how I can help] …." Sometimes, just listen. Don't talk at all.

(8) Share your challenges

Remember your children are meeting you as full-fledged adults post-career development. Particularly if you have a successful career, your children might not understand that you went through struggles. Conveying your challenges will alleviate their sense that they are failing.

Most parents tell success stories: "...and that's how I got my promotion". Or they do not convey the circuitous and sometimes challenging path that led them to their career. "I suffered and want to minimize the amount you suffer..." is one way to open with a discussion of your past challenges.

(9) Short regular discussions

The longer a topic is avoided, the more taboo it becomes. At least once a week, ask if you could help them or if there is anything they want to discuss will keep the conversation going. Blocking off three hours—unless agreed upon in advance—will likely not be fruitful.

(10) Guide effectively through imparting critical career counseling general principles

It may be a tall order to suggest that you become an expert on the New World of Work. But it does make sense to become reasonably conversant in concepts that will help your child. My hope is that this book provides one resource that will help you to do so.

PART II:

EXPLORATORY WORK:
THE PROCESS TO FIND A HAPPY
AND SUCCESS CAREER

OUR SCHOOLS, FROM K-COLLEGE, HAVE FAILED IN HELPING young people find well-matched careers. The lack of career exploration is the missing element underlying this failure. Most college graduates drift into their careers, in part because structured and meaningful career exploration is not an aspect of our education system. That makes you and your children responsible for creating your own career exploration projects.

But career exploration has a huge impediment. As noted earlier, the process and outcome are filled with ambiguity. Few are adept at putting in work that is both indistinct in process and indefinite in outcome.

Contrast learning how to drive with learning how to find a well-matched career. For new drivers, the process is clear: some form of driver's education that takes less than a couple of months. The desired outcome is singular, distinct, and finite: You will know how to drive.

The process of career exploration is broad, ill-defined and non-finite. What exactly does one do to search for a career? Moreover, there is no way to know with certainty that your judgment was correct prior to investing time and energy into the career path.

In addition, unlike new drivers who are more or less beginning at the same level, career seekers come from enormously different starting points. Some are confused but only in the narrowing of options—such as a business student choosing industry and functionality—and some are entirely clueless, in a literal sense expressing they have no idea what they want to do. Most disheartening of all, there are no definite outcomes or timelines. The career seeker does not know with certainty that she has it right until the first job experience (at least) and other than artificial deadlines such as declaring a major, there are wide variances in how long it takes to derive a satisfying career choice.

Nonetheless, there is no other answer for what one must do to find a career path. Exploratory work is not optional. It is required to take control of your career. Otherwise, your child will drift into a career and let fate decide whether it is a fit.

Moreover, while I know many parents want their children to "just get a job", having a "career vision"—the end result of exploratory work—is critical for career seekers to effectively and efficiently find a job. I often hear parents bemoan the lack of career motivation of their twentysomething. "He's not even applying for jobs…" That someone is not applying "for jobs" is not that surprising. Applying for jobs that are not part of a vision is exhausting and deflating. My twentysomething clients tell me they feel conflicted: "Do I really even want this job?" The lack of vision prevents them from directing their energy into a career search.

Career Exploration Creates A Compelling Career Vision

Those who have a "why" can bear almost any "how". Ask any would-be Marine going through boot camp why he is willing to do pushups in the mud. The vision of being a Marine is a powerful motivator. This wisdom holds true for those who are committed to distinct career paths as well. Distinct end goals will help your children develop the necessary skills to move toward a better path and deal with the initial drudgery that is part of almost all paths. The "why" inspires the "how".

Creating Your Own Exploratory Work Structure

What is exploratory career work? Exploratory work could be viewed as everything one does to evaluate careers before deciding on a career path. Many people do very little in this regard. You may also grow indignant when you think about how much time your children were compelled to spend in areas that had or will have no bearing on their career paths. How can it be that those who are certain they will never work in advanced math have to suffer through Algebra II and beyond, instead of spending time in a well-crafted career exploration program?

Why Exploratory Work Provides a Critical Advantage for Job Search

If your adult child is already done with the college, then there is one more huge advantage that Exploratory Work provides: focus. Those on the job/career hunt using a targeted rifle are at a serious advantage compared to those using the scattered shotgun approach. Looking for anything and everything usually leads to nothing.

When your children discover what they want, not only will they be able to precisely tell others their objective, which helps others help them, but their Reticular Activating Systems (the RAS is essentially our brain's search engine) will alert them to possibilities that lead to their goal.

How does this work? Once their RAS is activated in relation to a distinct career interest, all news items, conversations, and thoughts related to that interest will seem to magically appear. Those triggers were always present. Previously, they had filtered *out* instead of filtering *in* this information. Optimizing their RAS by deciding what to focus upon will maximize their energy both in a literal and abstract sense. Concentrating on distinct opportunities within a potential career field will yield better results than scanning online job boards for something that might fit.

Moreover, if they know what they want, they will be more effective in telling others who are in a position to help them. It is very hard to help people who want "a job." I have edited many resumes with vaguely stated objectives such as "a challenging job that is suited to my skills." If anything, this phrase tips off the reader that the applicant does not know what they want. It is far easier to help someone who wants "a marketing position in the biotech sector in Boston."

The College to Career Seeking Program

There is no singular way to find career happiness and success. Our College to Career Program, while a distinct process that works for many, is not the only way. When we work with clients—and I am highly self-conscious about appearing to advertise for our career program—we have a process that works but we still need to customize.

Going forward, I am shifting the book to speak directly to your child. Here's where you either need to work with them or have them work alone in order to tangibly start the process. Regarding the former, review the section on how to be a guide. Regarding the latter, realize that psychological blocks, as much as practical ones, prevent many from moving forward. Across all disciplines, coaching provides an accelerant to learning because of the coach's expertise in the former and application of techniques for the latter. Here, you are the coach.

The Career Seeking Program is broadly divided into three areas:

(1) **understanding you**

(2) **understanding the marketplace**

(3) **deciding optimal fit.**

UNDERSTANDING YOU

STEP 1:

SELF-AWARENESS

"KNOW THYSELF" IS THE FIRST TENET OF WISDOM FOR A WIDE swath of psychological and spiritual arenas. This is true in career exploration as well. The various methods designed for greater self-exploration often lead to greater benefits beyond career and work.

Since there is extraordinary variance in how twentysomething clients understand themselves in relation to the work world, career coaching needs to be customized. Some of our clients are highly self-aware. Some are lost. Most are still finding their way. Some are eager for exercises designed to discover what work suits them. Some get uncomfortable with self-reflection or anything that appears psychologically invasive. There is a gender difference here as men are often more resistant to self-discovery exercises. Nonetheless, I can provide one certainty: I have never worked with a twentysomething who did not discover something helpful when going through self-awareness exercises. Indeed, most made a few discoveries that were profoundly significant and some had life-changing epiphanies.

To start the process, here are the highly simplified definitions of components related to career self-awareness.

1. **Personality preferences:** *your natural tendencies*

2. **Values:** *what you care about*

3. **Core Motivations:** *your psychological needs*

4. **Interests:** *topics you enjoy*

5. **Aptitudes:** *your innate strengths*

6. **Skills:** *your developed abilities*

7. **Credentials:** *your resume*

8. **Life-situation:** *how career affects life outside of work*

   Geographical desires: *how where you want to live affects your career*

   Relational considerations: *how your career affects your relationships*

   Work-life balance: *how your career affects your personal life*

Personality Preferences:

Personality preferences are your natural tendencies. We generally like work that fits the way we are wired. The importance relates to what type of work activities and work situations suit us. Consider someone outgoing versus someone shy. Jobs that require networking, sales calls, and high interaction with new people would be heaven to one and hell for the other.

Those who are happy accountants and those who are happy advertising directors chose their work correctly because their work fits their natural tendencies, the former preferring distinct procedures leading to distinct answers and the latter preferring creative space for open-ended possibilities.

Some prefer solving analytical problems and others prefer connecting with others. Those who view research labs as fascinating are internally different than those who relish counseling others.

Some like distinct routines and deadlines. Others would chafe at such structure. The administrator who relishes ensuring the trains run on time is different than the EMT who thrives in not knowing what each day will bring.

Some people know themselves well and have the capacity to coherently narrate their preferences. Others could benefit from personality profiling tests.

A word on Personality Profiling Tests:
Personality tests are merely tools that help people understand their preferences. Those who are highly self-aware are often not surprised by the results. Moreover, there are other methods that can be used for those who immediately retract when presented with anything that appears less than rigorously scientific. Nonetheless, powerful personality profiling tests can lead to career and life-changing insights. Still, career tests do not reveal anything but data. That data must be turned

into information. And, that information must be turned into actionable advice. Otherwise, the tests are fun and somewhat interesting but otherwise useless.

Those who have been frustrated by career tests are usually expecting the tests to provide the "answer" to what they should for a career. No such test can do so. The tests are not endpoints, but rather starting points in helping you gather intrapersonal career wisdom.

Tests to Use

Which tests to use? There are many. Here are some common ones:

Myers-Briggs: provides information on one's natural personality preferences

Five Factors: focuses on the following major dimensions of personality: Openness, Conscientiousness, Agreeableness, Extraversion, and Neuroticism.

Strengths Finder: As its name implies, this test focuses on discovering the test-takers areas of strength.

O'Net (sometimes called RIASEC): focuses on finding which areas of interest best suit the test taker. Realistic, Investigative, Artistic, Social, Enterprising, and Conventional

Any of the above tests, and several others, can provide useful data. Moreover, none of these are mutually exclusive. Take all the tests if helpful and feasible. The most important aspect involves having a skillful interpretation of the data derived from the tests to turn into information that can be useful. Whatever test or tests you choose, do not use superficially or it will be a waste of time. Learn enough to interpret or get an expert to interpret.

I will elaborate on Myers-Briggs which I find—when understood—to be effective. The test is also the most easily accessible, as there are several reputable websites that provide the test for free. Do a quick Internet search and you will discover several free and effective options. Moreover, the results are reasonably easy to understand, and the one most likely for readers of this book to have taken. While it doesn't mean it is the best, Myers-Briggs is generally viewed as the most used career personality profiling tool.

> The test provides four areas of preferential variance:
> Extroversion-Introversion;
> Sensing v. Intuiting;
> Thinking v. Feeling
> and
> Judging v. Perceiving.

The end result is a four-letter combination such as ENFJ (my type, if you are curious). As is the case with all such boxes that attempt to capture human variance, there are dozens of nuances, exceptions, and subtleties that are required to account for the imperfectly fitted descriptions.

The test measures which direction we lean within the continuum of the dichotomous variables. The stereotype of the social butterfly and the bookworm would have percentages highly tilted in either direction of the extroversion-introversion continuum. Most people have more moderate differences. Those that are close on the scale between the two descriptors should note that the result might not provide a clear-cut preference. For example, the term "ambivert" is used to describe someone who is balanced on the extroversion-introversion scale. Such types can be the life of the nighttime party on the same day that they spent hours alone reading a book. If you take the test, pay special attention to areas where you have distinct preferences.

E) Extrovert vs. (I) Introvert

How we gain our energy

The standard definition: extroverts gain energy by interacting with people. Introverts need to recharge after being with people and gain their energy by being alone. Sales jobs—where chit-chat is required to develop rapport—would be a terrible fit for a high Introvert. But it is too simplistic to claim that jobs involving high interaction with people suit extroverts and jobs involving sufficient time alone suit introverts. For example, introverted scientists will thrive in jobs where they are working in teams that talk a great deal but only as long as the focus is about solving scientific problems. They will not thrive in jobs where they are forced to engage in small talk.

Introvert	Extrovert
Derive energy from inner world	Derive energy from outer world
Thinks—without talking—to clarify thoughts	Speaks to others to clarify thoughts
Prefer depth over breadth	Prefer breadth over depth
Initially seen as difficult to get to know	Initially seen as easy to get to know
Prefers to work independently	Prefers to work with others
More likely to have a few close relationships	More likely to have many relationships
Concentration on work activities is preferred	Interaction with others for work activities is preferred
Reflects before making decisions	Tends to make decisions quickly

(S) Sensing vs. (N) Intuitive

How we take in information

Sensors take in information via their five senses and through facts, and Intuitives take in information via patterns, impressions, and possibilities. Of the four dichotomies, this is the least inherently understood by most. Some generalities may clarify: Sensors prefer to learn through straight-forward approaches. Classes involving real-world applications be it in accounting, biology, and mechanical areas are often attractive to sensors. Classes involving theory and interpretation be it literature, psychology or philosophy are often attractive to Intuitives. As a simple test, ask a person to describe various rooms in their house. High Sensors are likely to readily give specific details. High Intuitives might pause and then provide some big picture descriptions.

Sensing	Intuition
Gather information through the five senses	Gather information through interpreting patterns
Thinks in the present	Thinks of future possibilities
Concrete thinkers	Abstract thinkers
Notices details	Sees big picture
Practical	Idealistic
Factual	Theoretical
Gather info from what they can see, hear, touch and feel	Gathers info from developing underlying patterns
Realistic	Inventive

(T) Thinking vs. (F) Feeling

How we make decisions

Thinkers make decisions based on facts, and feelers make decisions based on values. Note the terms have nothing to do with intellectual ability but rather how decisions are made. People commonly say thinkers use their heads more than their hearts and feelers use their hearts more than their heads. There is some truth to that claim.

I served as a criminal prosecutor in Philadelphia when I started my career. I soon understood that some judges preferred arguments that focused on the "relevant facts" within the four corners of the law and then rendered decisions accordingly. Fairness was paramount. Certainly, this approach has its appeal. But sometimes there were facts that either called for more toughness—let's say the crime was against a defenseless elderly person—or more mercy—let's say the defendant was retaliating for an attack on his brother - that Feelers would consider more strongly. With judges that I knew had a greater Feeling orientation, I would emphasize the context of the case. My favorite judge had a similar feeling orientation as I do. He could tell from my presentation whether it seemed that greater leniency or greater justice was required for particular defendants. With Thinking judges, I would focus on how the facts fit the statutory violation of the law. I felt more robotic. But one of these judges would often rebut the defense with a simple: "The facts are the facts. Nothing you or I can do to change them. Guilty."

In terms of jobs, as expected, nurturing professions such as counseling, are more suited for Feelers. Impersonal professions, engineers come to mind, are more suited for Thinkers.

Thinking	Feeling
Decides with analysis	Decides with feeling
Judge based on logical thought	Judge based on feelings
Driven by thinking	Driven by emotion
Critical	Empathetic
Truth	Tact
Impersonal	Personal
Not easily upset by others' remarks	Takes remarks personally
Rational	Passionate

(J) Judging vs. (P) Perceiving

Our lifestyle preference.

This dichotomy is the least accurately named. The term "Judgers" is a misnomer. It has nothing to do with making judgments or being judgmental. Similarly, the term "Perceivers" has nothing to do with being perceptive.

Judgers, in Myers-Briggs parlance, prefer their world to be structured, while Perceivers prefer their world to be open-ended. Judgers like plans. Perceivers find that plans are constraining. Judgers feel a sense of control in planning early and Perceivers find a sense of control in leaving their options open. For me, the most obvious way to test is the person's relationship to time. As someone who has an appointment driven calendar, I almost always can predict who will arrive on time and who will be late. Judgers take time seriously. Those with a high judging preference will arrive 10 minutes early. Those with a high Perceiving preference usually arrive late. Judgers tend to be more decisive as they prefer to close out options. Perceivers prefer to delay finalizing decisions as they like to keep all possibilities in the air. That might sound a bit too positive for the Judgers. So, let me also say that high-level Judgers tend to be inflexible and Perceivers, in general, are more spontaneous, and thus often, more fun.

Judging	Perceiving
Prefers to finish one job before starting another	Start many things without finishing
Moves towards closure	Keeps options open
Structured	Flexible
Prefers to plan before acting	Spontaneous with actions
Controlled	Relaxed
Organized	Disorganized
Follows plans	Tends to veer from plans
Responsible	Tends to procrastinate

Analysis of Your results:

If you take the test, you will get one of sixteen combinations. I am well aware of all the caveats. Most people do not neatly fit into boxes. The emotional health of someone and/or learned behavior will make people of the same type seem very different. For example, an undeveloped ENTJ will be domineering and autocratic. But a wise ENTJ will have either outgrown the worst parts of the type and/or learned that behaving in certain ways leads to problems. As such, they will have many of the attributes common to good leaders. In either case, ENTJs almost always have strong personalities and you can feel their presence. Moreover, many people are very balanced in one or more dimensions. It is relatively common for someone to have distinct preferences in a couple of areas but also have one or more that are essentially indistinct. In such cases, read both descriptions (i.e. an ISTJ who is almost equal on the extroversion scale should also read the ESTJ description to gather insights). Moreover, family and cultural upbringing affect the outward manifestation of the traits. Those with more exuberant cultures will often exhibit their traits more strongly than those from more muted cultures.

The four-letter combinations are described below:

ISTJ

Thorough, dependable, analytical, logical, practical, and realistic. Orderly, organized, follow procedures well. One of the most common types in our society. Stable career paths are valued. For that reason, many are attracted to jobs in large organizations or predictable career paths.

ISFJ

Quiet but friendly, responsible and kind, conscientious and caring. Order and harmony are highly important. Also, one of the most common types in our society. Service-oriented and stability driven. Often considered the backbone-nurturer in organizations.

INFJ

One of the least common types. Idealistic and seeker of meaning in relationships. Often self-conscious, feel misunderstood or different. Generally, not materialistic. Nicknamed the counselor. Happiest in careers that help people and serve the common good.

INTJ

Inventive, independent, critical. Original minds and great drive for implementing their ideas and achieving their goals. Quickly see patterns in external events and develop long-range explanatory perspectives. Skeptical, high standards of competence and performance for themselves and others. Prefer careers where they feel in control of their ideas.

ISTP

Rational, practical, fixers. Observers until a problem appears, then act quickly to find solutions. "Mechanic" is one nickname of this type. Analyze what makes things work and readily get through large amounts of data to isolate the core of practical problems. Interested in cause and effect, organize facts using logical principles, value efficiency.

ISFP

Quiet, friendly, sensitive, and kind. Desire creative freedom. Design-oriented. Enjoy the present moment. Like to have their own space and to work within their own time frame. Loyal and committed to their values and to people who are important to them. Dislike disagreements and conflicts, do not force their opinions or values on others.

INFP

True idealists who likely have a hard time finding a paying career path that is also emotionally satisfying. Loyal to their values and to people who are important to them. Seek to understand people and highly accepting of others. Unusual type and as such often feel misunderstood.

INTP

Absent-minded professors. Theoretical, often more involved in the life of the mind more than social interactions. Develop logical explanations for everything that interests them. Quiet, with a high ability to focus in depth to solve problems in their area of interest. Skeptical, sometimes critical, always analytical.

ESTP

Action, oriented, entrepreneurial types. Take a pragmatic approach focused on immediate results. Want to act rather than ponder theories. Focus on the here-and-now, spontaneous. Enjoy material comforts and style. Learn best through doing.

ESFP

Nicknamed the entertainer. Spontaneous, outgoing, friendly, and accepting. Enjoy working with others to make things happen. Bring common sense and a realistic approach to their work, and make work fun. Learn best by trying a new skill with other people.

ENFP

Idea generators who often lack follow through. Imaginative. See life as full of possibilities. Make connections between events and information very quickly. Like to keep options open. Dislike the mundane and are attracted to generating interesting ideas.

ENTP

Nicknamed "the debater", ENTPs are either appreciated for their provocative nature or problematic for those sensitive to being challenged. Stimulating and outspoken, adept at generating abstract possibilities and then analyzing them strategically. Good at reading other people. Bored by routine, and often able to master new areas when interested.

ESTJ

Clear, straightforward, usually interested in career paths with direct lines to the top of organizations. Organized, take care of details, logical, systems-oriented types. Practical, quickly move to implement decisions based on a systems approach. Organize projects and people to get things done, focus on getting results in the most efficient way possible. Often leaders in organizations.

ESFJ

Often in career paths where teamwork is valued as ESFJs are a nurturing type that desire bringing people together. Want harmony in their environment, work with determination to establish it. Like to work with others to complete tasks accurately and on time. Loyal, follow through even in small matters. Want to be appreciated for who they are and for what they contribute.

ENFJ

Seek to bring out the best in others. Idealistic, motivators who lead others through warmth and persuasion. Highly attuned to the needs of others. Find potential in everyone, want to help others fulfill their potential. May act as catalysts for individual and group growth. Sociable, facilitate others in a group and provide inspiring leadership.

ENTJ

Nicknamed the General. Confident, decisive, assume leadership readily. Can be tactless when being direct. Logical, efficient, solver of organizational problems. Enjoy long-term planning and goal setting. Forceful in presenting their ideas.

If you take the test, you will get one of the types. Regardless, in and of itself, the results will not be anything but mildly interesting to those interested in such assessments. The data needs to be converted into helpful information. For example, some readers will test out as INFPs. Introverted, iNtuitive, Feeling, Perceiving. The information needs to be explained. Collectively, and depending on how pronounced these preferences are within the Myer-Briggs methodology, INFPs are individualists and idealists. Still, even after explanation, this information is not useful. You need guidance on how to apply this information to your particular career.

A career counseling example:

A college junior who I will call "Sean" came in for career counseling. He was studying business, finance specifically, with the intention of gaining entry to a large corporate organization. He found himself miserable as he was interviewing for summer internships and envisioning a career in the business world.

As Sean walked in the doors of stodgy corporate behemoths, he felt ill at ease. He came to me because he was getting depressed about a career in corporate America. This surprised people who knew him superficially. He looked, dressed, and acted in a conventional manner. He came from a suburban, button-up, conservative family. He had attended an all-boys Catholic school and now attended a college that had a lot of conventional, preppy types. He certainly looked like he would fit into the corporate world. Nothing, at first glance, gave the impression that he was anything but as he appeared: a straight-laced, conventional, organizational type.

Sean's Myers-Briggs came back as an INFP. INFPs are among the least suited Myers-Briggs types for the traditional corporate world. (ISFPs and INFJs are the other types).

The corporate work world is antithetical to the personality preferences of those who are distinct INFPs. The following are generalizations and should be taken as such since plenty of individual counter-examples are true:

Extroverts fit in better at large corporations particularly at lower levels where small talk and other social superficialities are valued. Introverts can and do very well as deep problem solvers within such organizations. But they often struggle with corporate politics, face time, and cocktail parties.

Sensate types follow procedures and details better than Intuitive types. Since most entry-level jobs in large corporations require adherence to structure and processes, sensate types are less likely to forget to follow bureaucratic guidelines. Intuitive types are often the big visionary thinkers who do rise to the top of their fields. But, at least at the start of their careers, intuitive types often feel trapped, bored, and frustrated by the rules and red tape inherent in large organizations.

Thinkers are more naturally suited to large organizational culture because such cultures tend to be more head than heart-based. That's a broad statement that likely captures the IBMs better than the Patagonia's of the business world. Nonetheless, there are still more old school Fortune 500 companies than upstart new way of doing business entities. This also relates to work functionality as those in accounting are likely to be Thinkers and those in human resources are likely to be Feelers.

Judgers (those who like structure) are more suited to large organizations because Perceivers (those who like to keep options open) do not particularly like deadlines and routines, basically the way of life at large organizations.

None of the traits individually creates much of a problem for those in large organizations. But, collectively, the combination of all four less accepted traits make the INFP too individualistic and sensitive for many highly structured workplaces.

Sean was not surprised at all. He told me that he had adapted his outer image to fit in with both his family (he had two older brothers who were "athletic frat guys") and at his high school. Sean could fool almost anyone into thinking that he was one of the guys. But, he never felt that way. The thought of continuing this act into the work world was making him sick.

When I directed him to areas of business such as marketing, web design and the startup world, Sean was quite inspired. The test result seemed to give him permission to start exploring a different area business that would be more suited to him. Unleashed from focusing on finance, he decided to shift his energies toward marketing and thanked me profusely from saving him from career misery.

Values:

Career values relate to desired work outcomes and stem from one's philosophical outlook on life. For some, work is simply a way to pay the bills, and for others, a critical way to move towards self-actualization.

Discussion often gets undermined by not putting values in a prioritized list and not considering what you would give up in order to meet your dominant value. All things being equal, every rational capitalist would prefer a career that makes a lot of money to one that does not. But, all things are not equal, most jobs that pay a lot of money require long hours. Long hours affect work-life balance and family time. Some will take the trade-off and some will not. To really understand this point, consider the following: If you had a current salary at a job that was a pretty good fit that paid your bills with some savings left over and generally had hours of 9-6 pm, how much more money would it take to increase your everyday hours to 7 pm? 8 pm? 9 pm? One of my valued teammates, who loves his work, replied during his review: "I know I'm supposed to want to make more money. But I would be content making what I make now for the rest of my life." I told him that he has great clarity on his values. So, working more hours or doing other work that he would not enjoy as much in order to make more money did not make sense.

Similarly, many people say they want an exciting job. But exciting jobs usually come with high stress. Some profess a desire for a stress-free job but such jobs are usually boring.

After writing ten values, choose five. Then order each and determine if there is one dominant value at your current stage of life. For example, there are many in their twenties who would prioritize money and prestige over family and work-life balance. This may change over time. At the moment, focus on your current values. Here are a few common values but there are many and your values might be unique.

Financial success

Good benefits (health insurance/retirement plans)

Making a positive difference

Psychological fulfillment

Enjoying work activities

Work-life balance

Low stress

Security

Excitement

Control of time

Your unique values

Core Motivation

Those who enjoy self-reflection will relish this section and perhaps have an epiphany or two. Those who do not will find this section disconcerting. But this may be the most important "understanding you" aspect of the College to Career Program.

Most people do not unpack the "why" behind desires and more particularly what one will endure in order to get their desires met. While the reasons are often multi-faceted, there most often are only a couple of dominant drivers. If a client tells me they want to "get rich", I do not view the surface answer as the end of the conversation. I want to know why.

I come back to money a great deal in relation to work because financial need is one of the few commonalities for most all my clients. Some want to make a lot of money and are willing to make the trade-offs that will be required. Some want to follow their passion and just want to figure out how to make enough money to do what they want. And there are countless slices in between. Regardless, money is inevitably part of the work conversation and, for many young people, making a lot of money is important.

Some want to get rich to gain public approval. So, for instance, if the person was suited to the work and could become rich through a non-prestigious profession, such as plumbing, they usually balk. Legal careers provide a reasonable framework to understand this issue. Anonymous partners in New York law firms make at least five times more than Supreme Court Justices. Which job would you prefer?

Some want to get rich to feel free. They think of making as much money as possible so that they can quit. Thoughts of working in a corporate structure for decades in order to accumulate wealth sound akin to prison terms. Such types want to do their own thing. Getting rich means sitting on a beautiful beach and not having to answer to anyone. Given The New World of Work and the possibilities of working remotely while freelancing or creating a virtual business model, there are a growing number of young adults who are free from the confines of an office. Most are not getting rich, at least in the short term, but they have satisfied their core desire for freedom.

Others yearn for security. They feel safe knowing that they have enough money to avoid financial worries. I explained to one of my older clients who has a solidly paying federal government job that his pension was equivalent to a multi-million-dollar retirement nest egg. Moreover, the likelihood that he would get laid-off was minimal compared to those in the private sector. This went a long way to quelling his gripes that he made less money than others. He really just wanted to know that he and his family were secure.

Some want to be rich to feel special and show off their uniqueness. There are plenty of ways to distinguish oneself without making a lot of money. Some want to ensure they can provide for their family. Explaining that "being there" for your family is more important than providing a lot of money helps those who choose careers with more modest earning potential but that will enable plenty of family time.

And while many have a mixture of all of the above and more, there is usually one that is most significant. What is most important to us? This will often be the biggest determinant for why we act and what attracts us.

What's the difference between core motivations and values? The former relates to our deep subconscious wiring and the latter can usually be self-reported. For example, someone might report that she wants to have enough time to pursue her own interests. That's a value. The "why" behind that value is the core motivation. Those not well versed in the sub-conscious might be confused. But most understand the difference between someone expressing the desire for time freedom but who, when asked why, responds that she wants enough time to practice piano versus someone who expresses she hates the idea that an organization controls her free time. Suffice to say, understanding your core motivation can be highly relevant in making career decisions.

The most common core motivations:

The need to feel successful
The need to feel secure
The need to feel appreciated
The need to feel at peace
The need to feel in control
The need to feel free
The need to feel unique
The need to live with integrity
The need to feel capable

Again, it is likely that most everyone has some needs in each of these areas. Put these in order. For some, this exercise can be quite powerful in providing career guidance. If you want a powerful personality tool that can help you identify your core motivation, take a free Enneagram test.

C. Interests

What interests you? Focus on areas that have potential applicability to careers. Playing video-games, binge-watching shows, and hanging out with friends do not count! What subjects did you like in school? What do you like to discuss? Read about? This can be a frustrating experience as you may say, "I don't read, didn't really like much in school, and don't really talk about anything that relates to careers." In the defense of young people, those statements are also true of many responsible adults who have careers. So, there needs to be a process in place to determine interests.

Our College to Career Program uses a reading-research process to get concrete answers: There are business publications that discuss a wide range of industries. *Forbes, Fortune, The Wall St. Journal, Business Week,* and *The Economist* are publications that typically address big business. This is not to say that innovative companies and ideas are not mentioned but rather the focus of these traditional magazines usually deal with issues that affect the masses. Similarly, there are business publications that address the New World of Work more directly and, as such, have a more distinct focus on start-ups and small businesses. *Fast Company, Inc.,* and *Entrepreneur* are three publications that I recommend. While each currently has print editions, most twentysomethings would prefer perusing online. Moreover, there are countless resources describing different professions and jobs young adults can peruse.

Even if for twenty minutes per day, we'll ask our clients to review different reading material with the goal to simply discover what interests them. Our parent-clients are routinely surprised because they thought their children were apathetic about their career when it turned out that they were simply uneducated about career possibilities. Many of our young clients will identify different interest areas and accompanying career paths.

D. Aptitudes, skills, and credentials

Aptitudes, skills, and credentials are different areas and should be treated as such. Understandably, career seekers often are confused between the differences because there is often an overlap between the three. For example, someone with native mathematical ability will likely develop top math skills and will have credentials, be it top grades or a college major, in the area. Nonetheless, there are differences.

Aptitudes relate to natural potential.

Skills relate to trainable abilities.

Credentials relate to experiences.

Here's a real-life example from one of my career counseling clients: Dana had a natural ear for languages. When she started taking Spanish, she picked up the proper accent and grammatical differences far more quickly than her classmates. She also is adept at miming other accents. For example, although she doesn't speak French, she can put on a French accent very well and can do so for other languages as well. Dana has an **aptitude** for learning foreign languages.

Dana took many years of high school and college Spanish and also engaged in significant self-education until she spoke Spanish as well as most natives. After this training, Dana had the **skill** of speaking Spanish. Dana majored in Spanish, passed a Spanish fluency test, and scored top marks in Spanish. All of those external accomplishments are Dana's Spanish **credentials.**

One of the bigger mistakes young people—and older people make—is describing themselves as "not good" in an area where they have not been trained. Many people have natural abilities that were never developed. Lebron James focused his athletic abilities on basketball. Let's assume he has not been trained to play tennis but recently decided to learn the game. Would it be accurate to describe him as "not good" or "not good yet"?! This is the case with all of us in many work-related areas.

Others have skills, developed through hard work and good training, but do not have a high natural aptitude. Historically, there have been a few short and not particularly quick NBA players. They were, without exception, gym rats.

Whenever we find incompetent workers, they have the credentials but not the skills for the job. For example, my biggest hiring mistake was hiring a bookkeeper who had worked in the accounting department of a big company. He had been laid off from his previous job, which he claimed was due to typical corporate restructuring. Within a few weeks, I was astonished by his imprecise calculations (revealing mathematical aptitude that was low for an accountant) and procedural bookkeeping errors (poor skills). His credentials did not determine what he could do well. I heard through the grapevine that he now has a small cleaning business. He was an action-oriented guy who really liked fixing up his house. Although he had no credentials for this business, my guess is that he'll be far more successful in physical work since his natural aptitudes are more aligned.

Here's another example to elucidate the difference between the aptitudes, skills, and credentials and give hope for those who do not think have the experience-credentials to enter certain career paths. John was the landlord of one of our company's offices. He was a Depression-era child who never graduated high school. But he had a strong *aptitude* for numbers. His first real estate ventures were literally sketched out on the back of napkins and scrap paper. He developed the *skill* of understanding real estate finance and then due to having gone through numerous successful deals also had the *credentials* to claim real estate finance expertise.

This is a highly important issue in the New World of Work. Many people—not just underemployed twentysomethings—will note that they do not have the requisite experience to embark on a career path.

In the case of twentysomethings, they typically say that they majored in something dissimilar or that their internships or first jobs do not provide either the skills or the credentials for the career. I explain that they are being short-sighted. Skills, by definition, are only developed through education, training, or experience. John was not born with real estate finance skills but rather with an aptitude to understand the flow of numbers. Similarly, credentials are continually built through one's lifetime. John's credentials stemmed from moving from one deal to the next until he had successfully completed several multi-million-dollar deals. The high school dropout now had the same real estate financing skills and credentials as most real estate tycoons with Harvard MBAs.

The last three areas in our analysis relate to life-situation. These are highly important and often overlooked in career discussions.

Geographical desires: *where you want to live*

Relational considerations: *how your work affects your relationships*

Lifestyle factors: *how your work affects your personal life*

Geographical preferences

There are three dominant geographic considerations:

1) Living near "our" people

Young people want to live near their friends/girlfriends predominantly, and family in some cases.

2) Living in an area for social reasons and/or preferred things to do

A vibrant social scene—usually in cities—is often of high concern. Weather or other interest areas are important to some. Some of my clients want to be near the mountains because they are ski fanatics; while some in warm weather so they can golf all year.

3) Living in an area where the field they are in is dominant

Despite the increasingly online nature of our personal and work lives, geography still matters and, in some cases, a great deal. My would-be investment banking clients better be okay with living in a major city and best in New York. Political animals are best suited for Washington D.C. or state capitals and some industry hubs like Silicon Valley and Hollywood have made their geographical location synonymous with career paths.

Relational considerations:

Relational considerations have an obvious overlap with geographical considerations as living near "your people" is both a geographical and a relational consideration. But relational considerations include living in a place where your partner/spouse's career can also flourish. In addition, a career choice that takes time away from your spouse/children/parents might also not suit some. Those marine biologists who go away for six weeks often rethink their careers when they have children.

Work-life balance. Work-life balance was heavily tilted towards work for the prior generation. I recall one of my investment banking friends half-kiddingly explain that his employer seemed to figure out exactly how much money to pay to convince young bankers to give up another year of their twenties. There are still those willing to do so. But I hear with increasing frequency the desire of twentysomethings to have work-life balance. Some want enough time so they can pursue their hobbies. Some want a lot of free time regardless of whether they are using the time productively. Some want work-life balance as part of their principles for healthy living.

STEP 2:

PRIORITIZING AREAS OF SIGNIFICANCE

THE NEXT STEP WILL BE EASY FOR THOSE WHO ARE DECISIVE and brutally difficult for the indecisive.

Determine the dominant area or areas of significance. Plenty of clients emerge from these exercises and declare two or three important criteria and view all other information as helpful but not critical in their career considerations. Some, of course, are now overwhelmed with self-discovery data.

As referenced in the psychological challenges of 'The Perils of Choice', I Want it all, It Will Come to Me, and Analysis Paralysis, decisions about what to do will not be easy. Developing self-knowledge will be helpful. The goal, however, is not navel-gazing but rather action-oriented decision making: what really matters to you? More importantly, what trade-offs are you willing to make?

As noted, a common challenge is the desire for both a lot of money and a lot of free time for family and/or personal life. High paying, prestigious careers usually create a challenge for work-life balance. When I was in my twenties and practicing law at a large firm in Washington DC, I met with an older financial planner. In the context of discussing my potential income, I told him about why I was fairly sure that big law firm life was not for me. Given that it was in his interest to maximize my investing assets, I thought he would advise me otherwise. Instead, he asked me how important family was to me. Before I could answer, he said, "Everyone says that family is the most important thing but not many big law firm lawyers spend their time that way. When I meet with attorneys at large firms who are over 40, I generally assume that alimony and child support will be part of the process. Lots of people get divorced for all sorts of reasons but attorneys and investment bankers often get divorced because of their careers."

I told him that the two partners who hired me claimed that family was most important to them. One traveled over 200 days per year and the other would routinely say that the "real work begins after 5 pm." Maybe they were just deceptively selling me or maybe just deluding themselves but "family time" was not a priority in the way they lived their lives. Soon thereafter, I had lunch with a friend who worked with famed attorney Brendan Sullivan, best known for his role defending Oliver North during the Iran-Contra scandal. At the time, he was representing a large client in the mid-west in a multi-million-dollar trial. Sullivan, then in his mid-fifties, was at the top of the pack of private firm litigators. But, like my young law firm associate friend, was working twelve to fourteen-hour days and commuting weekly to the middle of the country from Washington, DC for the better part of several months. Sullivan is a master of his craft and I'm sure derived satisfaction from such immersion. But knowing that Sullivan's lifestyle would be the price to pay for such success helped crystallize my decision to leave big law firm life. Relationships were my dominant priority so leaving big firm law became easy enough after value clarification.

Go through all the self-discovery conclusions. Determine what matters most by placing those conclusions along the must-want continuum. Take out a big piece of paper. Write "Must" on one end and "Want" (as in nice to have but not necessary) on the other end. For example, some people might enjoy travel as part of a job but not view travel as critical for job happiness. That criteria would be closer to "Want".

STEP 3:

RESEARCH THE
MACRO-MARKETPLACE

WITH GREAT HOPE, MANY OF YOU CAN SKIP THE GENERAL OVERVIEW step because you have, at least some direction regarding areas of interest. For those who profess they have "no clue", there is a helpful process that we use.

Surveying the marketplace

The US government is quite good at gathering data. So, while there are other sources that provide a comprehensive list of career and job possibilities, the government's Business Labor Statistics provide a good place to start.

Here are the general categories that are listed for jobs in the United States from the US Government's Business Labor Statistics:

Management
Business and Financial Operations
Computer and Mathematical
Architecture and Engineering
Life, Physical, and Social Science
Community and Social Service
Legal
Education, Training, and Library
Art, Design, Entertainment, Sports, and Media
Healthcare Practitioners and Technical
Healthcare Support
Protective Service
Food Preparation and Serving
Building and Grounds Cleaning and Maintenance
Personal Care and Service
Sales
Office and Administrative
Farming, Fishing, and Forestry
Construction and Extraction
Installation, Maintenance, and Repair
Production
Transportation and Moving

Systematically go through areas that might be of interest. This is not as daunting as it may appear. Typically, clients only have 2-3 areas of real interest and even those who profess to know little about the world of work rarely review more than 5 general areas. Also note that, unsurprisingly, the government is a bit outdated in categorizing jobs. You have to click into broad areas such as "Internet" and "Business", among other areas, to find specific jobs

Upon choosing an area, you'll click through to a screen with more precise descriptions. For example, if you focus on the health care areas, you will see more precise descriptions of nurses, physician assistants, health care techs and so forth. From there, click further to get statistical data that will prove somewhat useful. More importantly, conduct further research in fields of greater interest.

The value of this exercise often stems from providing the range of options available within the general marketplace and descriptions of specific jobs. Many of our clients struggle because they are waiting for what I call "the mythical perfect career path." When they meet the actual job marketplace, they start to confront reality. As an example, my clients who profess an interest in law or law enforcement sometimes have a tangible option—such as lawyer, paralegal, police officer—that meets their needs. But some young clients want a made-up job such as a forensic specialist, who, while not being a police officer, solves crimes, or who, while not being a lawyer, provides trial strategy. Usually, this stems from watching too many TV shows! Explaining that most forensic specialists are lab technicians who simply report the results of tests to detectives and attorneys who handle the case from there may burst their bubble but also helps them move forward. Gaining an understanding of the reality of their options can be initially deflating but is wonderfully liberating in providing focus.

In addition, this exercise often compels young people to develop what many parents long for: a developed sense of financial reality. Sidney was an idealistic young twentysomething who attended an excellent liberal arts college. She also came from high affluence. She had intended to head into social work. But having never developed a concrete understanding of how salaries correlate with lifestyle was dismayed when she finally understood that a social worker's salary would not cover penthouse living in Manhattan. Surveying jobs in social work made her reconsider her career aspirations and we redirected our energies to finding work that suited her interest in working with people but also could generate a high income.

Geographical survey:

It is far easier to search for jobs in your geographic area than elsewhere. Search through a list of companies near you. Review job titles in the company. It doesn't matter if there are openings yet. Just find jobs and companies that you think would be of interest.

Relational survey:

It is also far easier to learn about—and often get—jobs through connecting with your friends, relatives, and acquaintances. Linkedin is currently the most professional way to build and tap into your network. But so is whatever social media list you have at your disposal. Go through a list of your contacts. As best as possible, determine what each person does and consider whether it is worth reaching out for a conversation.

STEP 4:

RESEARCH THE MICRO-MARKETPLACE

WHICH JOB CATEGORIES ARE WORTH GATHERING MORE DATA on? Research methods vary but web searches serve to gather preliminary information. Gather in-depth material to study the field. Ideally, this would include talking to others in the field of interest. Then reverse engineer what is needed for a successful career path. For example, I have had several clients consider the value of an MBA. If you examine the career paths of high-level management at Fortune 500 companies, you will see that MBAs are prevalent. If you examine career paths of high-level management in start-up companies, you will see proportionality fewer MBAs. My clients who envisioned careers in corporate behemoths could more readily see the value of MBAs compared to most others.

This is the stage where diving into specific areas is required. This demands deeper research and analysis. More importantly, speaking with someone in the field would be invaluable. When I train new entrepreneurs, I urge them to learn the "secrets of the marketplace" from someone who is in their intended business. So, for example, those who want to open restaurants usually have dreamed about the final presentation of a well-run fine eating establishment but, far too few have spent energy understanding the back-end operation as well as the financial considerations of restaurant ownership. I would be far more willing to invest in a restaurant with someone who understood how to effectively create a kitchen set up and where to purchase the best and most cost-effective food to prepare than someone who has a clever idea about menu items. The former understands the secrets of running a restaurant, the latter just the superficialities. The same holds true for any field.

STEP 5:

CREATION OF A "CAREER PILOT"

I USE THE TERM "PILOT PROGRAM" (LIKE A TV PILOT) AS THE END goal of career exploration. Thousands of television pilots are made each year. Those that succeed get purchased by network executives. Those that are purchased for one season still have to get renewed each year. Some turn into *Game of Thrones* and many disappear. So, it is with career exploration. The goal is to create an attractive enough initial option to take the first concrete step. You then might decide against taking another step. Or you might continue. The hope is that you'll find one that continues until you are on your path.

As for taking your first step, many of my career counseling clients have to be reassured that they are not locking themselves into forty years of work. I assure them that they are making small movements forward. This could include: (1) signing up for further training/education and/or engaging in a structured self-education program (2) filling out an application for graduate school or employment (3) meeting with someone in the field. I then note that, while I would not want them to change course because of small bumps, they always have the option to pivot. Just take the next step forward!

Thereafter, take one step after another until it is time for real commitment.

Pay-Your-Dues Work

Most fields require that you pay your dues. Such work creates the first real commitment. While it is disheartening that so many people get depressed when searching for suitable work, it is even worse that many people will not venture into fields that seem to suit them because they cannot muster up the energy to do the necessary, often challenging, preliminary work required.

I have had twentysomething clients express utter dismay in their current career path. They believed the new career path that we discussed held far better promise for their future happiness and success but would balk at venturing onto that path when they realized they would have to take a step down in pay or prestige. I understand the feeling. Taking one step backward—even if you know it will lead to two steps forward—is difficult in the short run. It is also necessary sometimes as the alternative is plowing ahead in a field that will cause certain unhappiness. Others would stop because they faced difficulty of one sort or another. But like anything worthwhile, difficulties are inevitable and investment—Pay-your-dues work—is necessary if you want to follow a new path. Those stories of CEOs who started in the mail room were about enterprising young adults who long ago paid their dues.

One common form of Pay-your-dues work is graduate school. Given the costs of higher education, I want to ensure my clients are committed to their chosen path before making such an investment.

But credentials and training are essential for some fields, and you can't become a doctor or lawyer without paying for and attending medical or law school. Similarly, for those interested in honing their skills or building their credentials, degrees, certifications, and classes will matter. You want to create a great app that helps save the planet by making consumers aware of their environmental footprint? You had better invest in learning how to code or get credentials sufficient to be hired by an app maker.

Other forms of Pay-your-dues work include internships, some of which are unpaid, entry-level jobs within an industry, and also may include taking second jobs to pay bills if part of the initial path does not provide sufficient income.

Once you have decided that your path is a suitable one, please— for the sake of your older self - do what is necessary to move forward.

On Your Path

After sufficient steps are taken and presumably some amount of "Pay-your-dues" work has been completed, you will be on your way. But some cautionary words designed to keep you moving would be wise to embrace.

Perfection is the enemy of the good. You may hear others describe the perfect college, the perfect spouse, and the perfect career. This may create the fear of missing out if you find that your intended career does not meet that impossible standard. Beyond the thought that most exaggerate the exciting and few advertise the mundane parts of life, even the most wonderfully matched college, spouse, and career pose challenges. Moreover, while I am not suggesting that you settle for something that is merely passable, I must relay a real-world truth: poll after poll reveals that the majority are unsatisfied with their work lives.

Just by having a "good enough" career, you are doing pretty well. My hope, of course, is that you have a great career. But if you have a career that is on the plus side of happy, consider yourself fortunate.

Embrace the challenges on your chosen path. Here's some counterintuitive wisdom: part of the satisfaction from reaching your career goal will be overcoming the problems on your path. Strangely enough, you will wind up happier because—not in spite of—those struggles. Those doctors who suffered through organic chemistry, lawyers who struggled through sadistic Socratic method questioning, and investment bankers who battled through differential calculus usually look back at their war stories with pride.

Do not confuse a situational challenge with one that condemns the whole career path. More than a few clients have overestimated the significance of a bad meeting or a bad class or a bad first job experience in relation to a career path. The "bad college tour guide" may be the most relevant metaphor. While I know that a tour guide might be indicative of the type of students at the college, it is beyond irrational when students dismiss colleges filled with thousands of students because they disliked their one tour guide, particularly when there is little indication that the guide was representative of typical students at the college or, more to the point, that they fail to consider that most colleges have students of many types. So, it is when career seekers have a terrible teacher in the field of interest or a terrible boss that ruins an internship experience and then dismiss the field entirely. I have had clients tell me that they loved the work of their internship but their mean co-worker made their work life unbearable and, for that reason, they are seeking a different career path. Unpack the experience. If you liked the activities, then you simply need to find work situations that fit your style.

Understand that work rewards—such as making a lot of money, getting a lot of time off, or having fancy titles—take far more time to attain than academic rewards. You won't get on the Dean's List at the end of a semester. You will not be up for promotion every year.

Patience is required. Work rewards take years, not months. I still work hard but I have had younger staff members comment on how lucky I am to take most Fridays off as well as long vacations. I remind them that they did not see the early years when I once worked 107 straight days and routinely worked 300 plus days of the year.

Luck and other factors not in your control are part of success. Your income will be, in part, related to short term factors out of your control, such as how the company is performing. Also, know that part of success comes from the luck of choosing the right ship. Some portion of those who became wealthy working at Google had applied for and were rejected for employment at Yahoo.

The energy required to find the right path will all be worth it. Nonetheless, the rewards for a well-matched career are well worth the energy required to find one. Life consists of time. Work takes up a lot of time, a lot of life.

I now am at age where I can make observational conclusions about what leads to happy lives. Health (physical/psychological), Relationships (family/friends), and Career (what we do/the results of what we do) are the big three for most.

I also know that if one area is a big problem, then the challenges from that area tend to color all aspects of life. Those with terrible careers usually report being unhappy, even if the other areas of their lives are solid. For that reason, do whatever you can to ensure your career is at least "good enough."

I can also say—delightedly—that those who get "career" right go a long way towards having happy lives beyond the compartmentalization of work happiness. Having a happy career will certainly help you stay psychologically fit and seems to correlate, and perhaps cause, efforts to stay physically healthy. Moreover, there is no question that having a happy career leads to having better relationships. Coming home in a good mood will make you a better spouse, parent and friend.

Most importantly, if you are spending a large chunk of time –for most half of one's weekday waking hours—at work then it is reasonable to conclude that a happy career often equals a happy life.

CONCLUSION

WE ARE LIVING IN RADICALLY CHANGING TIMES. THOSE WHO
live in the midst of revolutions have amazing opportunities and perilous
challenges. My earlier career guidance book, *Career Path of Abundance*,
focused on the opportunities that exist for young adults to create far
happier and more successful career paths than those of prior generations. This was not a universally rosy prediction. I noted that the amazing possibilities described were for the well-credentialed, highly skilled,
self-motivated types who no longer have to wait in line to start companies, build organizations, and launch new ideas.

This book was designed to address parents of those outside the
thin slice described above. That phrase "Path of Abundance" came
from my first book, *Motivate Your Son*, which described three paths
that I foresaw most of the next generation heading into: The Path of
Abundance, The Path of Struggle, and The Path of Disaster. I estimated
that 10% would be on the Path of Abundance and that seems to be about
right. Most will be struggling, and, unfortunately, this generation will
have more who will not be financially independent than any generation

in recent history. To help the next generation of children, we parents must contribute longer than many of us expected.

That you are continuing to help your children into adulthood does not mean you are overbearing but, instead, heroic. Many parents—energy drained—give up. You, however, have taken the time to go beyond what most parents do.

I salute you in your quest.

ABOUT THE AUTHOR

Daryl Capuano is the CEO of The Learning Consultants and its subsidiary Career Counseling Connecticut. Daryl has been advising adults on their career counseling needs for over a decade. Daryl's path from Ivy-league lawyer to education-entrepreneur stems from following his own practical-idealist career process for building a career that leads to happiness and success. Unlike most career counselors who have minimal experience in different industries and in management roles, Daryl has served on hiring committees of various private and public organizations. As the CEO of The Learning Consultants, the largest private education consultancy in Connecticut, Daryl is involved in hiring on a weekly basis.

The combination of counseling experience blended with a deep understanding of how the real world works makes Daryl's approach to career counseling unique. Recently named to *Who's Who in America* and author of *Motivate Your Son* and *Career Path of Abundance*, Daryl speaks on education issues at the local and national level. Daryl graduated *magna cum laude*, Phi Beta Kappa and first in his concentration from Georgetown University. He then earned a joint JD-MGA from Penn Law School and Penn's Fels School. Daryl also earned a prestigious Equal Justice Foundation Fellowship, for which he served at The Brookings Institute, the nation's top think tank. Daryl lives in Old Saybrook, Connecticut with his wife and three children.

To contact Daryl directly: call 860 510-0410 or e-mail: dcapuano@learningconsultantsgroup.com See also: www.learning consultantsgroup.com and www.careercounselingconnecticut.com